The Vanishing Race

The Last Great Indian Council

Joseph K. Dixon

Alpha Editions

This edition published in 2024

ISBN : 9789362920218

Design and Setting By
Alpha Editions
www.alphaedis.com
Email - info@alphaedis.com

As per information held with us this book is in Public Domain.
This book is a reproduction of an important historical work. Alpha Editions uses the best technology to reproduce historical work in the same manner it was first published to preserve its original nature. Any marks or number seen are left intentionally to preserve its true form.

Contents

The Concept .... - 1 -
PERSONÆ .... - 3 -
INDIAN IMPRINTS A GLIMPSE BACKWARD .... - 6 -
THE STORY OF THE CHIEFS .... - 39 -
THE STORY OF THE SURVIVING CUSTER SCOUTS .... - 115 -
THE INDIANS' STORY OF THE CUSTER FIGHT .... - 131 -
THE LAST GREAT INDIAN COUNCIL .... - 153 -
INDIAN IMPRESSIONS OF THE LAST GREAT
COUNCIL .... - 160 -
THE FAREWELL OF THE CHIEFS .... - 171 -

The Concept

In undertaking these expeditions to the North American Indian, the sole desire has been to perpetuate the life story of the first Americans and to strengthen in their hearts the feeling of allegiance and friendship for their country.

For this purpose two expeditions were sent forth to gather historic data and make picture records of their manners, customs, their sports and games, their warfare, religion, and the country in which they live.

As a result, on Washington's Birthday, 1913, thirty-two Indian chiefs, representing eleven tribes, assembled with the President of the United States together with many eminent citizens and details from the Army and Navy to open ground for the Indian Memorial authorized by act of Congress to be erected in the harbour of New York.

The Indian chiefs assembled, hoisted the American flag, the first time in their history. This act and the flag gave birth to a thrill of patriotism. These warriors of other days laid claim to a share in the destiny of our country. So deeply were these First Americans impressed with a sense of loyalty to the flag that, again under the authority of the President of the United States, a third Expedition was sent forth to every Indian tribe. The purpose of this Expedition was twofold, the linking of every tribe in the country with the National Indian Memorial, and the inspiring of an ideal of patriotism in the mind of the red man—a spirit of patriotism that would lead to a desire for citizenship—a feeling of friendship and allegiance, to be eternally sealed as a convenant in the Indian Memorial.

Here, under the blessing of God, on the shores of our beloved country, where the red man first gave welcome to the white man, this Memorial will stand in eternal bronze, in memory of a noble, though vanishing race, and a token to all the world of the one and indivisible citizenship of these United States.

RODMAN WANAMAKER.

The Approach of the Chiefs

PERSONÆ

Representative North American Indian Chiefs, scouts, and warriors participating in the Last Great Indian Council, held in the valley of the Little Horn, Montana, September, 1909, with their English, tribal, and Indian designations.

CHIEF PLENTY COUPS, Chief of the Crow Nation, bearing the Indian name of Aleck-shea-Ahoos, signifying Many Achievements.

CHIEF RED WHIP, an eminent Chief of the Gros Ventres Tribe, bearing the Indian name of Bein-es-Kanach.

CHIEF TIMBO, OR HAIRLESS, Head Chief of the Comanche Tribe, bearing the Indian name of Tah-cha-chi.

CHIEF APACHE JOHN, an eminent Apache Chief, bearing the Indian name of Koon-kah-za-chy, signifying Protector of his Tepee.

CHIEF RUNNING BIRD, an eminent Chief of the Kiowa Tribe, bearing the Indian name of Ta-ne-haddle.

CHIEF BRAVE BEAR, Head Chief of the Southern Cheyennes, bearing the Indian name of Ni-go High-ez, Ni-go, bear—High-ez, brave.

CHIEF UMAPINE, Head Chief of the Cayuse Tribe, bearing the Indian name of Wa-kon-kon-we-la-son-mi.

CHIEF TIN-TIN-MEET-SA, Chief of the Umatilla Tribe, bearing the Indian name of Wil-Lou-Skin.

CHIEF RUNS-THE-ENEMY, Chief of the Teton Sioux, bearing the Indian name of Tok-kahin-hpe-ya.

CHIEF PRETTY VOICE EAGLE, Chief of the Yankton Sioux, bearing the Indian name of Wambli-ho-waste.

CHIEF WHITE HORSE, Chief of the Southern Yankton Sioux, bearing the Indian name of Sung-ska.

CHIEF BEAR GHOST, Chief of the Crow Creek Tribe, bearing the Indian name of Mato-Wanagi, signifying the Ghost of a Bear.

CHIEF RUNNING FISHER, an eminent Chief of the Gros Ventres Tribe, bearing the Indian name of Itn-tyi-waatyi.

BULL SNAKE, an eminent Crow warrior and scout, bearing the Indian name of Ear-Ous-Sah-Chee-dups, signifying Male Snake.

MOUNTAIN CHIEF, Chief of the Blackfoot Tribe, bearing the Indian name of Omaq-kat-tsa, signifying Big Brave.

CHIEF RED CLOUD, Chief of the Ogallalla Sioux, bearing the Indian name of Marpiya-Luta.

CHIEF TWO MOONS, Head Chief of the Northern Cheyennes, bearing the Indian name of Ish-hayu-Nishus, meaning Two Moons or Two Suns.

WHITE-MAN-RUNS-HIM, Chief of the Custer scouts, an eminent Crow warrior, bearing the Indian name of Mias-tas-hede-Karoos, signifying The White Man Runs Him.

HAIRY MOCCASIN, a noted Custer scout, of the Crow Tribe, bearing the Indian name of Esup-ewyshes.

CURLY, a noted Custer scout, of the Crow Tribe, bearing the Indian name of Shes-his.

GOES-AHEAD, a noted Custer scout, of the Crow Tribe, bearing the Indian name of Basuk-Ose, signifying Goes First.

A Glimpse Backward

INDIAN IMPRINTS A GLIMPSE BACKWARD

We are exchanging salutations with the uncalendared ages of the red man. We are measuring footsteps with moccasined feet whose trail leads along the receding sands of the western ocean. A bit of red colour set in immemorial time, now a silent sentinel, weeping unshed tears with eyes peering into a pitiless desert.

Life without humour is intolerable. The life of the Indian has been a series of long and bitter tragedies. There is a look in his face of bronze that frightens us, a tone lights up the gamut of his voice that makes it unlike any other voice we have ever heard—a voice that will echo in the tomb of time—a Spartan courage that shall be regnant a millennium beyond the Thermopylæ of his race.

We have come to the day of audit. Annihilation is not a cheerful word, but it is coined from the alphabet of Indian life and heralds the infinite pathos of a vanishing race. We are at the end of historical origins. The impression is profound.

A vision of the past and future confronts us. What we see is more wonderful than a view the points of which can be easily determined. We behold a dead sea of men under the empty and silent morning, a hollow land into which have flowed thousands upon thousands—at last the echo of a child's cry. The door of the Indian's yesterdays opens to a new world—a world unpeopled with red men, but whose population fills the sky, the plains, with sad and spectre-like memories—with the flutter of unseen eagle pinions. A land without the tall and sombre figure worshipping the Great Mystery; without suns and snows and storms—without the scars of battle, swinging war club, and flashing arrow—a strange, weird world, holding an unconquered race, vanquished before the ruthless tread of superior forces— we call them the agents of civilization. Forces that have in cruel fashion borne down upon the Indian until he had to give up all that was his and all that was dear to him—to make himself over or die. He would not yield. He died. He would not receive his salvation by surrender; rather would he choose oblivion, unknown darkness—the melting fires of extermination. It is hard to think this virile, untamed creation has been swept like hurrying leaves by angry autumn gusts across the sunlit plains into a night without a star.

The white is the conquering race, but every-whither there is a cry in the heart to delve into the mystery of these ancient forerunners. This type of colour holds the eye, rivets and absorbs the interest.

Men are fast coming to recognize the high claim of a moral obligation to study the yesterdays of this imperial and imperious race. The preservation of this record in abiding form is all the more significant because all serious students of Indian life and lore are deeply convinced of the insistent fact that the Indian, as a race, is fast losing its typical characters and is soon destined to pass completely away. So rapidly are the remaining Western tribes putting aside their native customs and costumes, their modes of life and ceremonies, that we belong to the last generation that will be granted the supreme privilege of studying the Indian in anything like his native state. The buffalo has gone from the continent, and now the Indian is following the deserted buffalo trail. All future students and historians, all ethnological researches must turn to the pictures now made and the pages now written for the study of a great race.

It is little short of solemn justice to these vanishing red men that students, explorers, artists, poets, men of letters, genius, generosity, and industry, strive to make known to future generations what manner of men and women were these whom we have displaced and despoiled. Indisputable figures, the result of more than five years of painstaking research on the part of the Bureau of Ethnology at Washington, place the decrease of Indian population in the United Sates, north of Mexico, since the coming of the white man, at 65 per cent. They have gone from the forests and plains, from the hills and valleys over which they roamed and reigned for uncounted ages. We have taken their land, blotted out their faith and despoiled their philosophy. It has been the utter extinction of a whole type of humanity. The conquering Anglo-Saxon speech has swept out of existence over a thousand distinct languages. These original Americans *Deserve a Monument.* They have moved majestically down the pathway of the ages, but it culminates in the dead march of Saul.

The record of the North American Indian has naught to do with the tabulation of statistics, the musty folios of custom reports, the conquests of commerce. He has never walked up to the gates of the city and asked entrance to its portals, nor subscribed himself as a contestant in the arena of finance. He has had no share in the lofty ideals of statecraft, nor the spotless ermine of the judiciary. He lived and moved and had his being in the sanctuary of the hills, the high altar-stairs of the mountains, the sublime silences of the stately pines—where birds sung their matins and the "stars became tapers tall"; where the zitkadanto—the blue bird—uttered its ravishing notes. He sought the kat-yi-mo—the "enchanted mesa"—as the place of prayer, the hour in which to register his oath. On the wide extended plain, rolling green, like the billows of the ocean, he listened for wana'gipi tah'upahupi—"the wings of the spirits." In wana'gi ta'canku—the milky way—he saw the footprints of departed warriors. His moccasined feet penetrated wa-koniya—"the place where water is born"—the springs that gushed forth to give life, and refreshing to all the earth. Canhotka ska—the "white frost"—became the priest's robe as he petitioned at the sacrament of winter. The universe to him became a sounding-board of every emotion that thrilled his being. He found in its phenomena an answer to his longings and the high expression of every fervour of his soul. We cannot understand this, because the Indian chased the ethereal, the weird, the sublime, the mysterious: we chase the dollar. He heard the voice of nature; we listen for the cuckoo clock of commerce.

The Sacrament of Winter

The camera, the brush, and the chisel have made us familiar with his plumed and hairy crests, but what of the deep fountains of his inner life? What did he think? How did he feel? What riotous impulses, or communion with the Great Mystery, carved his face of bronze? These no scientist, no discoverer, no leader of expeditions have ever borne into the light. No footprints along the trail can spell out for us his majestic mien, his stolid dignity, his triumphant courage, his inscrutable self-poise, and all of these dyed with a blood-red struggle for survival such as crowns no other page of American history.

To gain this close measure of the Indian mind, his friendship and confidence must not suffer eclipse. It is a superlative task, for the inner Indian shrine is crossed by only a favoured few. The Indian is averse to being photographed, for he feels that every picture made of himself by so much shortens his life. He looks at his portrait, then feels of his person; he realizes that he has not lost a hand or a foot, but feels most profoundly that his soul will be that much smaller in the future world. His medicine is sacred, and you may not interrupt the daily tenure of his life without destroying some ceremonial purpose. It is meaningful, therefore, that these red men allowed us daily communion. This story is then simply instinct with the Indian's inner self: how we sat with him in his wigwam, and amid his native haunts, surrounded by every element of the wild life we were to commemorate; how his confidence was gained, and he was led to put aside his war-shirt and eagle feathers, and pull in twain the veil of his superstitious and unexplained reserve and give to the world what the world so much craves to know— what the Indian thinks and how he feels.

Memorable hours these under clear Montana skies, or at the midnight hour by the dim campfire light, the rain beating its tattoo on the tepee above our heads—surrounded by an army of shining tepees, like white ghosts of the plains, while these pathetic figures told the story of their lives. The warrior of other days gave himself up to mirthful tale, to boyhood's transports, to manhood's achievements, to the wild chase of the hunter, to the weaponry and woes of savage warfare, to the hallowed scenes of home life, to the primitive government of the tribe, and the busy and engaging activities of the camp; finally, to the royalty of the Great Council, when the chiefs assembled in solemn conclave to hold communion, to say a long and last farewell.

The Lone Tepee

Months of arduous labour were spent in the effort to make a comprehensive and permanent record of an old-time Indian council. For this purpose eminent Indian chiefs were assembled in the Valley of the Little Big Horn in Montana, from nearly every Indian tribe in the United States. This council involved permission and unstinted aid from the Bureau of Indian Affairs at Washington, the cooperation of the Indian superintendents on all the reservations; the selection of the most distinguished chiefs—chiefs eminent for ability and honourable achievement among their tribes. The council involved the necessity of interpreters from each tribe, for they could only talk in the sign language. It involved the construction of a primitive council lodge along the lines of history and tradition, and again, the reproduction of primitive customs and traditions, both in paraphernalia, costume, and conduct.

These imprints are the trail marks left by this Great Council of Chiefs—the last Great Indian Council that will ever be held on American soil. The story most faithfully records the idiom and phrasing and atmosphere of the Indian's speech as it came from Indian lips. The language of the landscape where the Indian made his home, where he fought his battles and lived his life, where this solemn council was held, is manifest in the accompanying photogravures. On the Indian trail, we may note as a hint of the many, a few of his imprints.

Singing to the Spirits

HIS RELIGION

The life of the Indian is one vast and glittering mosaic of rite and ritual. His warfare, his dress, his medicine, his ceremonies, his wooing, and his dying are all of them expressive of a dominant idea that pervades his life and controls his purpose. He lives constantly and absorbingly in a mystic land. He is beckoned by unseen hands and is lured into the realms of mystery by the challenge of voices silent to all other ears. His dress is studded with resplendent colours significant of the green earth, the blue sky, and the cry of his soul for a place in the great beyond. Like the high priest of old, he wears on his breast the fiery filaments of his faith.

The Indian sits in the tabernacle of the mighty forest or on the heights of some deserted and wind-swept mesa, beats his tomtom or drones song upon song, prays to the Great Mystery, pleads with the fires of the sun to give him strength and life and health, and calls the sun his father. The whispering winds tell his tale to the clouds. He peers into the depths of the stars, watches the aurora as the death dance of the spirits, answers the high call of the thunder as the voice of the Great Mystery, utters the cry of his soul to the lightnings—the arrows of taowity—communes with the rivers and the lakes, the moon, and the legion of wild beasts, and all of it with a pitiful longing that his days of fasting and his vicarious devotion may bring upon his life and his tribe the favour of the gods.

These primitive men hold time and money and ambition as nothing. But a dream, or a cloud in the sky, or a bird flying across the trail from the wrong direction, or a change of the wind will challenge their deepest thoughts. To the Indian mind all signs are symbolic. Their ceremonies are as complicated as any of ancient Hebrew or Greek tradition. The Indian aspires to be a great hunter, he seeks fame as a noble warrior; he struggles for the eagle feathers of distinction, but his greatest longing is to become a Medicine Man and know the Great Mystery. All medicine people of the tribes carry on their necks, or in a pouch at the belt, some sacred thing used in their magic practices—the claw of a bear, the rattle of a snake, a bird's wing, the tooth of an elk, a bit of tobacco. Every Indian carries his individual medicine, and his medicine is good or bad according to his success. If he finds a feather at wrong angle in his path, his medicine is bad for that day. The Indian fasts and dances and chants, using his mind, his spirit, and his body as pliable instruments in the making of his prayer. He finds in the veritable exhaustion of his body the spirit path made clear for his dreams, until the very stars seem as the eyes of the gods, and the sighing of the pines comes to him as the rustle of eagle wings to bear his spirit to loftier realms. Instead of the common acceptation that the Indian has no religion whatever, every single act of his life carries with it some ceremonial function, and his whole being is surrounded by a shining host of ceremonial spirits. The Indian goes with prayer thoughts to the water. His bath is a sacrament. He cuts the long supple willow withes that grow on the banks of the stream, enters the sharpened end into the soil, bends and ties the feathery tops into an arch; over the arches thus made he throws his blankets; meanwhile, gathered stones have been heated in the burning fire. These stones glowing white with heat are placed in a tiny pit underneath the covering of this booth, now to be called his sweat bath. First one stone until four have been counted are placed by the attendant in the pit, and then the fiery pile is thrown in promiscuous fashion on the heap. The Indians enter the closed covering, the ceremonial pipe is smoked, a gourd of cold water is handed to each; they then disrobe, the attending priest lowering the blanket over the entrance. Cold water is then poured over the heated stones, filling the enclosure with steam. In silence they commune with the Great Mystery until one of their number is blessed with a vision; then a call is made and the attendant lifts the blanket, almost immediately lowering it again. This action is repeated until the vision has been vouchsafed four times, when they all come forth and plunge into the river. These sweat baths are always located on the banks of a flowing stream. The Indian sees in every ripple of the flashing water that comes to meet him a shining token of the medicine he has seen in his vision. They then repair to the wigwam and listen in solemn silence to the chanting cadences of the Indian who has been favoured.

The Voice of the Water Spirits

The curling smoke from the long-stemmed pipe breathes forth the fumes of war or the pale quiet of peace. With his pipe he pacifies the elements. On festal occasions, or when the camp rejoices at the joys of harvest, the priest smokes his pipe, blowing the smoke first to the earth, then to the sky, to the north, the south, the east, and the west, in token of gratitude for the favour of the gods. With the pipe the Indian also seals his councils.

Trail of the Death Spirit

The Indian buries his dead upon some high elevation, because it is a nearer approach to the spirit world. They bury on scaffolds and in trees that in some mute, sorrowful way they may still hold communion with their loved and their lost. At the grave they go to the four points of the compass and mourn, singing all the while a weird chant. They bury with their dead all of the belongings of the deceased, the playthings of the Indian child, for the Indian boy and girl have dolls and balls and baubles as does the white child: you may see them all pendent from the poles of the scaffold or the boughs of a tree. When the great Chief Spotted Tail died they killed his two ponies, placing the two heads toward the east, fastening the tails on the scaffold toward the west. The war-bonnets and war-shirts are folded away with the silent dead; then follow the desolate days of fasting and mourning. In some instances hired mourners are engaged, and for their compensation they exact oftentimes the entire possessions of the deceased. The habitation in which the death occurs is burned, and many times when death is approaching the sick one is carried out so that the lodge may be occupied after the loved one has been laid to rest. The grief of the sorrowing ones is real and most profound. They will allow no token of the departed to remain within sight or touch. In their paroxysms of sorrow the face and limbs are lacerated, and often the tips of fingers are severed. Until the days of mourning are over, which is for more than a year, they absent themselves from all public gatherings. The bereaved fold themselves in a white blanket, repair to some desolate hillside overlooking the valley, the camp and the distant weird scaffold, and sit, amid cloud, sunshine, and storm, with bowed head, in solemn silence. White blankets are worn by the mourners as they move through the camp, significant of the white trail of the stars whither the Indian feels his loved ones have gone.

The Indian has a sublime idea of creation. He loves the brown earth and calls it his mother, because it has creative power and because it nourishes. And thus we might gather in from the thirty-two points of the compass the forces operant in earth and sky, and each would become a herald of the Indian's life of faith.

A Leaf from the Indian's Book

THE BOOKS OF HIS LIBRARY

The Indian child is nursed on Indian song and story. Tribal traditions are handed down from age to age by enacting in the dance, on the part of the warriors and braves, their deeds of valour in war, their triumphs in the chase, their prowess against all foes. Forest lore is a constant text book. He is taught to observe which side of a tree has the lightest bark—which side the most branches; why the tree reaches forth longer arms on the edge of the wood than in the depths of the forest where his eye is taught to penetrate. The squirrel, the rabbit and the birds all become his little friends: where and how they get their food, their manner of life, their colour, and how they call their mates, who are their enemies, and how they may be protected. His ear is trained to hear sounds ordinarily inaudible, his nostrils are early taught to distinguish the scent of the different wild animals. Then came his ability to imitate the call of this wild life, sometimes by direct vocalization, or by placing two reeds to the lips so dexterously that the timid fawn is led to his feet. This literature the Indian child studies, until his arms are strong enough to bend the bow and send an arrow speeding to its mark. He soon essays the rôle of a warrior. His study of the birds enables him to find the eerie of the eagle, for a victory means that he may add an eagle feather to his war bonnet or coup stick. His study of the hills enables him to find in their vermilion and golden seams the colours for his war paint. In the crimson berries festooning the banks of the stream, when crushed, he finds still another element of decoration. The white man makes a book whose leaves talk. The sunshine bears speech and light to the Indian. He lives by communion with the stars. The Great Bear of the stars is called the great animal of cold weather. When a shadow crosses his mind he watches the clouds that touch the moon when it is new. He reads the stars, for they travel to him in a familiar pathway across the sky. They are bright spirits sent earthward by the Great Mystery, and when thick worlds gather in clusters, there are so many souls of earth people that their trail makes luminous the white way of the sky. The wing of a bird is the symbol of thoughts that fly very high. From the bird that soars nearest the blue he plucks prayer feathers. These he dyes and cherishes with jealous care. The Indian possesses a strange love for growing things, tall grasses with lace-like plumes forming a lattice for the deep green of the slender bushes that bear the rich clusters of crimson buffalo berries. He knows and loves the wild flowers that hang their golden heads along the banks of the purling stream or that in gleaming colours enamel the wide stretches of the plain. There are a thousand leaves in every book, and with every book in nature's library he is familiar to the point of success.

The Song of the Arrows

HIS ADORNMENT

To the casual observer the costume and character of the Indian all look alike. The mind is confused amid a riotous and fantastic display of colours. The fact is that the minor details of Indian dress are an index to Indian character and often tell the story of his position in the tribe, and surely tell the story of his individual conception of the life here, and what he hopes for in the life hereafter, and like the laurel wreath on the brow of the Grecian runner, they spell out for us his exploits and achievements. To the white man all these decorations are construed as a few silly ornaments, the indulgence of a feverish vanity, but they open like a book the life of the Indian. His motive in adornment is to mark individual, tribal, or ceremonial distinction. The use of paint on the face, hair, and body, both in colour and design, generally has reference to individual or clan beliefs, or it indicates relationship, or personal bereavement, or is an act of courtesy. It is always employed in ceremonies, religious and secular, and is an accompaniment of gala dress for the purpose of honouring a guest or to celebrate an occasion. The face of the dead was frequently painted in accordance with tribal or religious symbolism. Paint is also used on the faces of children and adults as a protection from wind and sun. Plucking the hair from the face and body is a part of the daily program. The male Indian never shaves and the beard is a disgrace. A pair of tweezers becomes his razor. Sweet grasses and seeds serve as a perfume. Ear ornaments are a mark of family thrift, wealth or distinction, and indicate honour shown to the wearer by his kindred.

Among the Plains Indians the milk teeth of the elk were the most costly adornments. They were fastened in rows on a woman's tunic and represented the climax of Indian fashion, the garment possessing a value of several hundred dollars. Head bands, armlets, bracelets, belts, necklaces, and garters of metal and seeds and embroidered buckskin were in constant use. They were not only decorative but often symbolic. Archaeological testimony tells of the almost general use of sea shells as necklace ornaments, which found their way into the interior by barter or as ceremonial gifts. The chiefs of the tribe were fond of wearing a disk cut from a conch-shell, and these were also prominent in religious rites, ranking among the modern tribes as did the turquoise among the people of the Southwest. A necklace of bear claws marks the man of distinction, and sometimes was worn as an armlet. In the buffalo country the women seldom ornamented their own robes, but embroidered those worn by the men. Sometimes a man painted his robe in accordance with a dream or pictured upon it a yearly record of his own deeds, or the prominent events of the tribe. Among the southern tribes a prayer rug was made on deer skin, both the buffalo and deer skins having been tanned and softened by the use of the brains taken from the skull of the animal. The skins were painted with intricate ornamentation, symbols and prayer thoughts adorning the skin in ceremonial colours; white clouds and white flowers, the sun god, and the curve of the moon with its germ of life, the morning star, and also a symbol of the messengers from the gods. Above it all zigzag lines ran through the blue of the sky to denote the lightning by which the children above sent their decrees to the earth children who roamed the plains.

An Imperial Warrior

Footgear often proclaimed the tribal relation, the peculiar cut and decoration of the moccasin denoting a man's tribe. The war-shirt was frequently ornamented to represent the life story of the man wearing it. The breast contained a prayer for protection, and on the back might be found woven in beaded tapestry the symbols of victory. He had conquered the trail behind him. The shirt was often decorated with a fringe of human hair, the more warlike appending the scalps of the slain. The warrior wore no regalia so imposing as his war-bonnet with its crown of golden eagle feathers. Before the coming of the horse the flap at the back rarely extended below the waist, but when the warriors came to be mounted, the ruff of feathers was so lengthened that when the Indian was dismounted it trailed on the ground. The making of a war-bonnet was accompanied by song and ceremony. Each feather before it was placed in position was held in the hand and had recounted over it the story of some war honour. A bonnet could not be made without the consent of all the warriors and it stood as a record of tribal valour and a special mark of distinction granted to the man by his tribe. Every Indian takes great joy in laying out his colour scheme. It becomes a mosaic of artistic talent. Feathers are gathered from the eagles' flight. Skins are taken from the wild beasts. Bones, beads, sparkling metals, soft-tinted sea shells, and all of them blended with the varicoloured paints that he has compounded in nature's mortar. The woman enters into the work with intelligent zest, and when completed the whole array of blended colours is beyond the criticism of the tribe. The back of an Indian's war-bonnet and war-shirt is always more gaudy and sumptuous than the front view and this because when Indians pass each other their salutation is brief and formal. They ride right on. But after the meeting they turn in the saddle and look back to take an inventory. The wealth of the Indian, his position in the tribe, his ceremonial attainment are all passed upon and estimate entered. This colour scheme goes on through the entire Indian wardrobe to pipe sack, coup stick and moccasins. The Indian could not have received his suggestion for a colour scheme from the tinted leaves of autumn for they are dull in comparison. He may have had a hint from the glowing sunsets that in that western land fill earth and sky with a glory so transcendent that mere rhetoric is a profanation. More likely is it that when free and unrestrained he roamed over plain and hill his soul became enamoured with the dazzling array of colours, beyond the genius of the proudest palette, to be found in the marvellous formations that surround the great geysers of the Yellowstone, colours more exquisitely beautiful than the supremest refinement of art. Every-whither down the cone-shaped mounds are tiny steam-heated rivulets interlacing each other, edged with gold and vermilion and turquoise and orange and opal. Indian trails have been found also interlacing each other all through this wonderland. Deep furrows in the grassy slopes of these ancient footprints are still plainly visible. Thither we may believe came the red man imbued with the spirit of reverence and awe before all this majesty and beauty, and from this exhaustless laboratory claimed the vivid colouring for the expression of his life of faith.

A Sunset in Camp

Lighting the Smoke Signal

HIS WARFARE

The Indian has lived such a life of hazard for long centuries that he has had trained into him a first great instinct to fight. They have a war star in the sky, and when it moves the time to make war is heavy upon them. There are many cogent reasons for the belief that before the coming of the white man there were no general or long-continued wars among the Indians. There was no motive for war. Quarrels ensued when predatory tribes sought to filch women or horses. Strife was engendered on account of the distribution of buffalo, but these disturbances could not be dignified by the name of war. The country was large and the tribes were widely separated. Their war implements were of the crudest sort. A shield would stop a stone-headed arrow, and it necessitated a hand-to-hand conflict for the use of a flint-headed lance and the ponderous war club. The white man came, and for hundreds of years their contest has been waged against a superior force. They have disputed every mile of territory which has been acquired from them. During all that time they could not make a knife, a rifle or a round of ammunition. Their method of communication was confined to the smoke signal, signal fires and scouts. They had no telegraph, no heliograph, no arsenal. Modern implements of war they have been able to obtain only in late years and then in meagre quantities, even then only by capture or at exorbitant rates. The Indian has proved himself a redoubtable and masterful foe. For more than three hundred years millions of civilized white people have fought a bitter battle with three hundred thousand red men. During all these tragic years the nations of the world have moved on to discovery, subjugation, and conquest. Nation has taken up arms against nation. England, France, and Spain have put a rim of colonies about the globe. Our own great civil struggle has been written down on the pages of history with letters of blood. England, France, Spain, and the United States have during this period tried their prowess with these less than three hundred thousand braves and only now has the decimation become complete. No such striking example of endurance, power of resistance, and consummate generalship has been recorded in the annals of time. Sitting-Bull, Red Cloud, Looking-Glass, Chief Joseph, Two Moons, Grass, Rain-in-the-Face, American Horse, Spotted Tail, and Chief Gall are names that would add lustre to any military page in the world's history. Had they been leaders in any one of the great armies of the nation they would have ranked conspicuously as master captains. The Indian, deprived of the effectiveness of supplies and modern armament, found his strongest weapon in the oratory of the council lodge. Here, without any written or established code of laws, without the power of the press and the support of public sentiment, absolutely exiled from all communication with civilized resources, unaided and alone, their orators presented the affairs of the moment to the assembled tribe, swaying the minds and wills of their fellows into concerted and heroic action. The wonderful imagery of the Indian orator—an imagery born of his baptism into the spirit of nature—his love of his kind, and the deathless consciousness of the justice of his cause made his oratory more resistless than the rattle of Gatling guns, and also formed a model for civilized speech. It was an oratory that enabled a few scattering tribes to withstand the aggressions of four great nations of the world for a period of several centuries, and to successfully withstand the tramping columns of civilization. The science and art of Indian warfare would take volumes to compass. His strategy and statesmanship compelled victory. He was almost always assured of victory before he proceeded to battle. He knew no fear. A thousand lives would have been a small gift had he the power to lay them on the altar of his cause. He pitted the perfection of details against the wily strategy of his own colour and the pompous superiority of the white man's tactics. On the trail care was taken to cover up or obliterate his footprints. When a fire became necessary he burned fine dry twigs so that the burning of green boughs would not lift to the wind an odour of fire, nor carry a trail of smoke. He conceived and carried out a wonderful deception in dress. In winter a band of warriors were painted white. They rode white horses and their war dress was all of it made of the plainest white so that a group of warriors, stationed on the brow of a hill, would appear in the distance like a statuesque boulder clad in snow. This disguise also enabled them to come with stealthy step upon wild game. In autumn their horses were painted yellow and they wore a garb of yellow so that fringing the edge of the forest they could not be distinguished from the leaves of the dying year. The blue-green of the sagebrush, so conspicuously omnipresent on the prairies, furnished the Indian with another helpful form of disguise. He would almost completely disrobe and paint his face, his arms, and his hair, as well as the body of his horse, exactly the colour of the sagebrush; and when scouting, after their crouching fashion, among the clusters of sagebrush, or riding in the distance along the verdure-covered banks of a stream, the disguise would be so absolutely complete that detection became a difficult task. It was an ingenious and artistic display of war talent.

Answering the Smoke Signal

We are led to wonder often concerning the Indian's passion for his coup stick (pronounced coo). This rod, bedecked with eagle feathers and his own colour scheme, is the Indian's badge of empire. It is the "Victoria Cross" of his deeds of valour. In battle he rushes amid his foes, touches the enemy with his coup stick—that man is his prisoner, and he has counted a coup. He slays an enemy, then rushes up and touches him with the stick, takes his scalp; another coup is counted. The credit of victory was taken for three brave deeds: killing an enemy, scalping an enemy, or being the first to strike an enemy, alive or dead; any one of these entitles a man to rank as a warrior and to recount his exploit in public; but to be the first to touch an enemy is regarded as the bravest deed of all, as it implied close approach in battle. In the last Great Indian Council and on the journey home the attention of the writer was called to the prominence given to the coup stick. They are present at all ceremonial functions and are carried on all ceremonial parades. The warrior who can strike a tepee of the enemy in a charge upon a home camp thus counted coup upon it and is entitled to reproduce its particular design in the next new tepee which he made for his own use, and to perpetuate the pattern in his family. The eagle feathers on the stick can only be placed there after the warrior has counted his coup, recounted it in public, and the deed has met with the approval of all the warriors. The eagle, the proudest and most victorious of birds, then yielded a feather, which is deftly fastened with a circle of shining beads to the stick, and the proud victor flaunts another emblem of his bravery.

The Attack on the Camp

The buffalo, once the king of the prairies, has been practically exterminated. Perhaps no greater grief has ever entered into the life of the Indian than this wilful waste and irreparable loss. To this hour the Indian mourns the going away of the buffalo. He cannot be reconciled. He dates every joyful and profitable event in his life to the days of the buffalo. In the assembly of chiefs at the last Great Council the buffalo was the burden of every reminiscence. These veteran chiefs studied with melancholy eyes the old buffalo trails, and in contemplation of the days of the chase they said, as they thought backward, "My heart is lonely and my spirit cries." So much did they love the buffalo that the Indian children played hunting the buffalo. The animal furnished food and clothing, and many parts of the stalwart frame they counted as sacred. The annihilation of these vast herds aroused the darkest passions in the heart of the Indian, and many times stirred his war spirit and sent him forth to do battle against the aggressors. Within the nine years between 1874 and 1883 over eight millions of buffalo were ruthlessly slain. But the war curtain of the Indian has been rung down, and the vast area which twoscore years ago supported these vast herds of wild game is covered to-day with domestic animals and teems with agricultural life, furnishing food supplies for millions upon millions all over the civilized world.

Buffalo Thundered Across the Plains

An Indian Home

HIS HOME LIFE

Far stretches of prairie, winding watercourses, leagues of white desert with only the clouds in the sky and the shadow of the clouds on the blistering sand, an army of buttes and crags, storm carved, forests whose primeval stillness mocks the calendar of man, the haunts of the eagle, the antelope, the deer and the buffalo—and the edge of the curtain is lifted on the land where the Indian roamed and where he made his home.

Game has been found, a semi-circle of cone-shaped tepees dot the green of the plain; a stream, tree-fringed, fresh from the mountains, flows by the camp—a camp that in earlier times was pitched upon some tableland as an outlook for the enemy, white or red. Horses are browsing near at hand or far afield; old warriors and medicine men sit in the shade and smoke the long-stemmed, red sandstone pipe, and tell of the days of yore. Gayly clad figures dart hither and yon as the women are bent upon their tasks. Great loads of wood are brought into camp on an Indian woman's back. She carries water from the river, bakes the cake, upturned against the fire, boils the coffee and then all are seated on the ground when they partake of jerked beef, coffee, bread, and berries. Hands are better than knives and forks, one cup answers for many, and the strip of dried beef is passed along that all may cut off his desired portion. A noisy, gleeful group of children play with their dolls and their dogs—dogs that are made to serve as beasts of burden and instruments of torture. At night beds are made on the ground around the interior circle of the tepee and the chill of frost is driven out by a fire in the very centre— the most perfectly ventilated structure in the world—the air passing underneath the edge of the tepee in the loop where it is tied at the bottom of the poles, then passing on out through the opening at the top, carrying with it all dust and smoke. The Indian never knew anything about tuberculosis until the white man confined him in log cabins where a score of people live in one room, the cracks and keyhole entirely filled, and where they breath each other over times without number. Within the tepee the chief has the place of honour. A rest is made with supports like an easel. A lattice-work of slender willow rods passed down the front, which is covered by a long strip of buffalo hide. Against this the chief rests. Each member of the family has his allotted place inside the lodge and he may decorate his own section according to ability or fancy. Here the warrior hangs his war-bonnet and sometimes records his achievements in the chase or on the warpath. Lying all about the circle are many highly coloured parflesche bags containing the minor details of dress or any personal possession. Many of the tepees in an Indian village are embellished with Indian paintings setting forth the heroic deeds of the warriors who abide in the lodge. The figures are often grotesque and without parallel in the realm of art. The medicine is given a conspicuous place in the lodge. No one sits or lies down on the side of the tepee where they have placed the medicine of the household, and when they pass it on entering or leaving the lodge all heads are bowed. The medicine tepee is distinct from all others. It is painted a maroon, with a moon in green surrounded by a yellow circle. The medicine of the ordinary Indian family is hung over the entrance of the doorway or suspended on a pole, and may consist of a wolf skin or a dark blanket rolled in oblong fashion containing the sacred tokens of the family. Every Indian family takes pride in the ownership of a bevy of dogs. They are rich in dogs. In our camp of about thirty tepees a reliable Indian estimated that there were over three hundred dogs. These canines have free run of the lodge, and at night they crawl in under the edge of the canvas and sleep by their Indian master. Let an intruder enter the camp during the hours of darkness and they rush out simultaneously, howling like a pack of wolves until one might think the bowels of the earth had given forth an eruption of dogs. The Indian warrior makes a companion of his dog, and he can show no greater hospitality to a guest than to kill his favourite friend and serve his visitor with dog soup. To refuse this diet is an insult most vital.

An Indian Burden Bearer

The Indian woman is master of the lodge. She carries the purse. Any money that comes into the hands of the husband is immediately handed over. The servile tasks of the camp are performed by the women. Herein we have an expression of the law of equality. The husband has to perform the exhausting and dangerous task of hunting wild game for food and the skins for clothing.

He had to protect the camp against hostile attacks, and the woman felt that her task was easy in comparison. The Indian child rules the family. They are rarely, if ever, corrected. No Indian mother was ever known to strike her child. If they want anything they cry until they get it—and they know how to cry. In play they are as mirthful and boisterous as any white child. They ride mock horses, and play mud ball. The Indian boy prepares willow sticks, peels off the bark, then rolls the wet clay into balls, and, sticking the ball on the end of the twig, he throws it at a mark with great speed and accuracy. Perhaps the most popular sport among the children is what they term the stick game. Again willow rods are used without the bark, only this time they are cut short enough to be rigid, and they drive them with great velocity up an inclined board. When the stick leaves the board it speeds like an arrow far in the distance. Every Indian boy and girl owns a pony, from which they are almost inseparable, and which they ride with fearless abandon.

An Indian Woman's Dress—Mrs. Wolf Plume

While men are off in search of game the women make bead work of a most bewitching order, meanwhile watching the pappoose, fastened completely in its wooden bead-covered cradle, only the head protruding. The cradle is hung from a lodge pole or the bough of a tree, rattles and bells playing in the breeze. Other women gather in the shade and play the game of plum stone, a gambling game. They use the stones of the wild plum, which they colour with fanciful devices, and toss them up in a wooden bowl.

The Flower of the Wigwam

The wooing of Indian lovers varies with the tribes. One pair of lovers seal their vows by standing a little removed from the parental lodge, with a blanket covering their heads. In another tribe the negotiations are made entirely through the parents, when the transaction resolves itself into a barter, so many ponies for a bride; while in still another tribe, when a love fancy strikes a young man, he arranges to meet the young woman who has attracted him as she goes to the river for water. They pass each other in the path without any recognition. This occurs two or three times. Finally if the young girl welcomes these attentions she looks toward him as they pass. That night he comes to the lodge of her parents, remains outside, beating a tomtom and singing the love song. The young girl then goes out to meet him and they sit outside and talk. The next morning the mother asks her daughter about the affair, and then the mother invites the young man to come and dine with them and sit around the campfire. Thus the courtship proceeds until he finally says, "I will take this girl for my wife," and the two go to their own lodge. The Indian has an unwritten code of family morals to which he most rigidly adheres. In some tribes no Indian will cross the threshold of another if the wife of that man is alone, and in others no brother goes into the house where his sister is unless she has a companion. This is an ancient law and belongs to many tribes. The Crows have an eccentric custom that a sister after marriage is not allowed to be seen in public with her brother. Should an Indian alienate the affections of the wife of another Indian or steal his horse the injured one would be justified in taking his rifle and killing the offender. The whole camp would sanction the action on the ground that it would rid the camp of bad blood.

Little Friends

The Indian's civility and hospitality, both to his own kind and to strangers, has been a marked feature of his character from the coming of the white man to the present day. When Columbus touched the shores of the New World the friendly Caribs gave him hearty welcome. The heart's right hand of fellowship was stretched out in welcome and hospitality as explorers and settlers landed on American soil. Dignity, generosity, and courtesy marked the attitude of the Indian toward these new white strangers. The character generally attributed to the Indian is that of a savage, but this blemish came upon him through contact with the white man. Their ingenuous and trustful nature quickly degenerated as they were enslaved, betrayed, and slain.

Advantage was taken of their ignorance and kindness. Then came on a race war unparalleled in ferocity and barbarism. The inexorable march of civilization regardless of ethics swept on until we heard the Indians' war cry and failed to see the diviner grace of friendship. The Indian returned with interest every injury and hardship, every bitter assault and wicked aggression. He paid in full all accounts in the coin of pitiless revenge. These shadows obliterate our thought of him as courtier and hospitable host. The Indian will divide his last crust and then go hungry himself that you may have his half of the crust. Had it not been for Indian generosity in furnishing supplies of food, the early settlers in both New England and Virginia must have perished with hunger. Every guest entering an Indian wigwam is met by all the graces of hospitality—in cordial greeting—in a splendid home feeling.

A Bath in the Little Big Horn

Indian trails are no longer worn deep through the prairie sod, they have been growing ever more dim and indistinct. It is to-day, the "thin red line," a swift gathering of all that is left, in the gloaming, after the sunset.

The Crown of Eagle Feathers

THE STORY OF THE CHIEFS

The American mind could conceive a republic but not an Indian. America could conquer the Old World and rise redeemed and victorious when rent by the awful whirlwind of internal strife. But the red man defied her. His call rang across the plain like an autumn storm through the forests, and his fellow red men answered like clustering leaves. History shudders at the tale. Now look over the shoulder. When the fiery tongue of the Revolution blazed into the undying speech of liberty, Madison, Mason, Patrick Henry, and Edmund Randolph uttered their declaration that like a sunbeam has been written upon every page of the nation's history: "All men are by nature equally free and have inherent rights—namely, the enjoyment of life and liberty, with the means of acquiring and possessing property and pursuing and obtaining happiness and safety." Upon the inviolability of this sublime doctrine the early colonists fought for liberty, and the nation flung a battle line more than two thousand miles long, and engaged at arms over two millions of men, in order to procure liberty for another race. Once again, set each luminous word in this declaration over against the disposition and destiny that we have imposed upon the North American Indian. And then picture these famous Indian chiefs, gathered from many widely scattered wigwams; hear again and for the last time a life story that rounds itself out into an epic of sorrow; listen for the heavy footfalls of departing greatness; watch the grim faces, sternly set toward the western sky rim, heads still erect, eagle feathers, emblems of victory, moving proudly into the twilight, and a long, solitary peal of distant thunder joining the refrain of the soul—and it is night.

Warriors of Other Days

Chief Plenty Coups

Chief Plenty Coups

Chief Plenty Coups, chief of the Crow Nation, was exalted to the head of all the Crows because of his untarnished valour on the field of battle, because of the supremacy of his statesmanship, and his loyalty to the interests of his tribe. He derived his name, "many coups," from the fact that he was able to add eagle feather after eagle feather to his coup stick, counting coups in victory. When a lad of sixteen his brother was killed by the Sioux. The boy, bewildered with grief, climbed for two days, struggling to reach the summit of some high peak in the Crazy Mountains, there to give vent to his grief and pray for revenge. While he prayed to the sun he mutilated his body. Upon those lonely heights, never before desecrated by human footsteps, he dedicated his life to battle. Before he was twenty-six he had counted a coup of each kind and was made a chief, and named "Many Achievements." At sixty-three years of age he stands as erect as a solitary pine on a lonely hill crest. He has the bearing and dignity of a royal prince and wears his honours and war dress with all the pride and courtliness of a patrician. He glories in the fact that from his earliest days he has never fought the white man, but his life has been a long series of conflicts with other Indian nations. Before the white man ever placed his footsteps upon Indian soil his days were filled with struggle in warding off the blows of hostile tribes who sought the women and the horses of his own people. Then, to use his own expression: "The Great Father ordered that we should stop fighting and live in peace, and since that time we have had allotments of land, schools have been built for the education of our children, and as an illustration of the feelings of my heart to-day, I am at peace with all the tribes, they are all my brothers, and I meet them all as one man. I shall live for my country and shall remain in peace, as I feel peaceful toward my country." The reign of this great chief over his tribe is one of benignity and beneficence. He is greatly concerned in his last days to raise up young men who shall know the rights and opportunities of his people and who shall thus have influence at Washington, which he has many times visited and where he is always welcome. The smile of Chief Plenty Coups is worth crossing many miles of prairie to see. It was eminently fitting that this great chief on the grounds of his own Indian tribe should receive the chiefs attending the last Great Indian Council.

The Peaceful Camp

Chief Red Whip

Chief Red Whip [1]

Chief Red Whip is considered by his tribe as one of the greatest of the old hunters and warriors. The varying fortunes of the Gros Ventres, the strenuous war career of this noted chief, have ploughed deep furrows and written serious lines in his face. He is too old a man at fifty-five, but wounds and scars and battle rush age upon any man.

Chief Red Whip said to me: "The greatest event in my life was my fight with the Sioux in the Little Rocky Mountains. There were eleven Crows and three Gros Ventres in our band; our leader was a Crow. There were about one hundred and thirty Sioux. We were making the ascent of the Little Rockies, and my friends went down into the ravine to shoot some buffalo. While they were down there shooting the buffalo and cutting them up the leader sent me to do scout work. While I was up on the hills I saw the Sioux sneaking up to where we had killed the buffalo. I ran down at once to my friends and told them. We went back a little ways and made a fort and got ready to fight. I was painted yellow and red and was naked. When the fort was finished I went myself, taking two others with me, to find out the location of the Sioux. We went right up to where I saw them last. I could tell by their tracks that there were a great many of them. I went up a little ridge that divided our band from the Sioux, and just as I stuck my head up above the grass they all fired at me, about a hundred guns, but they did not hit me. When my friends heard the firing they came to where I was, and we went right down on the Sioux, and the Sioux came at us, and we had a fight for a few minutes at close quarters. After we had a short fight we rushed right on to the Sioux and they retreated. The Sioux had to go up a hill and we wounded some and killed others. After the Sioux had got up the hill I was the first one to get to a man who was killed. I scalped him and claimed everything he had. After the Sioux found out that we were only a small band they rushed down upon us and we retreated to where we had made the fort. Inside this fort there were two Crows killed with one bullet. The leader of the Sioux band was Chief Flying Cloud. I found out afterward who he was. It was Flying Cloud that we killed coming up the hill; he was trying to protect his band. When we were in the fort the Sioux people surrounded us. After the two Crows were killed the leader of our band became scared. I jumped out of the fort and led the way for my band. We ran the Sioux back to the Little Rockies, and then I told my friends to escape. As we retreated the Sioux pursued us. One Sioux was in advance and called upon me to stop, and as I stopped he fired at me but missed me, and then I fired and killed him. The Sioux then rushed on me so that I could not scalp the Sioux I had killed. We ran on into the mountains and escaped into another fort. In this last fort one of the Gros Ventres was shot and wounded. After we had rested a while the Sioux surrounded us again, and I rushed out at the Sioux so that my friends might escape again. While we were retreating again the Sioux shot one of the Gros Ventres through the leg, and he had to crawl on his hands and knees. I stayed with this wounded man, and the rest made their escape. I took this man on my back and carried him to some water at the head of a coulee. This Gros Ventre told me to go on and make my escape and leave him alone to die. While we were resting in the weeds at the washout the Sioux surrounded us again and waited for us to show ourselves. While we were waiting my wounded friend gave me his knife and paint and told me to tell his mother that she might have all his horses; then I jumped out and ran to catch up with my friends. After I had left my wounded friend about a quarter of a mile I looked back to see how the Sioux would treat him. There was one shot fired, and they all jumped into the washout, and then I made my escape. This gave me a great name in my tribe and among the Sioux and the Crows."

The Pause in the Journey

"Once on Tongue River there was a white soldier of the United States troops whom the Indians called Bear Shirt; he wore long hair like Custer. I was with him scouting for him. We called him Bear Shirt because he used to wear a bear coat. We came upon a band of Sioux, and there was a fight. This was a long fight, and there were many killed on both sides. In this fight when the Sioux got the best of the soldiers and the soldiers retreated, I stayed behind to protect them. The soldiers were so tired they could not run, and the Sioux killed off those who were too tired to run. I remained in the rear to protect them until they came to the main body of troops. When we were rested we went back to the main body of the Sioux and had another long fight and fought until sundown. There were a great many killed on both sides. We camped right where we quit fighting. The next morning we started to fight again and fought all day; again many were killed on both sides. The next day we went over the two battlefields and gathered up the dead soldiers and buried them. These battles were on Tongue River. After we had buried the soldiers I came back with the rest of the troops as far as the Yellowstone, and then went home." And yet such heroisms wrought out in lonely mountain fastnesses or on sun-parched plains will go unhonoured and unsung.

Chief Timbo

Chief Timbo

Chief Timbo, known as Tah-cha-chi, or Hairless, ranks as one of the leading chiefs of the Comanche Indians. With his stature of more than six feet, he is a commanding figure among any Indians. The portrait of Timbo reveals the striking difference to be found in the physiognomy of the southern tribes as compared with the northern tribes of the Plains Indians. In the photogravure presented Chief Timbo holds a long steel-headed spear, girdled with varicoloured beads, ornamented with great tufts of eagle feathers, and at the end of its ten feet of length bearing a picturesque plume. This staff descended to Timbo from Quanah Parker, once the leading chief of the Comanches. Chief Timbo brought this insignia of office from the southland to the council of the chiefs. In his own tribe the possession of such a mace answers among the Indians for the sceptre of a monarch. It is a coup stick with manifold emphasis. Chief Timbo accompanied the Kiowa, Cheyenne, and Apache chiefs to the council. They came as brothers, but no fierce fighting among these warlike tribes found a stronger or more fearless foe in the days gone by than this stalwart chief. In the assembly of the chiefs he moved among his fellows with a solemn and ponderous dignity, always silent and full of commanding reserve. In the battles that raged over the southern plains even far to the north, between the Comanches and the fierce Kiowas, Chief Timbo led his fighting bands to certain victory. Fierce blood runs in the veins of this masterful man, and only within recent years, and then not easily, has he submitted to Government rule.

The Downward Trail

Chief Apache John

Chief Apache John

The very name Apache means enemy and stands on the pages of all Indian history as a synonym for terror. Since our knowledge of them, the Apaches have been hostile and in every conflict they were favoured with rare and gifted leadership. It required the skill, strategy, and profoundest generalship of two of the greatest generals of the Civil War to subdue and capture the daring and reckless Geronimo, whose recent death closed the final chapter of a long line of unspeakable Apache atrocities. Koon-kah-za-chy, familiarly known as Apache John, because of his surrender to civilization, visited the last Great Indian Council as a representative of one of the many groups of this great body of Indians scattered through the southwest. There is an indefinable air of stoicism in the demeanour of all of these great chieftains. The subject of this text is not lacking in this prominent Indian element. A keen and piercing eye, a sadly kind face, a tall and erect figure, Apache John bears his sixty years of life with broad and unbending shoulders. He was fond of becoming reminiscent and said: "The first thing I can remember is my father telling me about war. We then lived in tepees like the one in which we are now sitting. We were then moving from place to place, and the old people were constantly talking about war. That was the school in which I was brought up—a war school. We kept on moving from place to place until I grew to manhood. Then I came to see a real battle. The first time I was in a battle I thought of what my father had told me. He told me to be a brave man and fight and never run away. I think this was good fighting, because I know what fighting meant from what my father had told me. At that time if an Indian wanted to win distinction he must be a good man as well as a good fighter. I was in a good many battles, until finally I had to give up fighting. About seven years ago the Government gave me advice, and with that advice they gave me different thoughts, and to-day I am one of the head men among the Apaches. I am head chief among the Kiowa-Apaches and I counsel peace among them. I used to think that my greatest honour was to be won in fighting, but when I visited the Commissioner in Washington he gave me other thoughts and other ways of thinking and doing until I felt that the new kind of life was the better. When the Commissioner told me these things I wrote them down in my mind and I thought that it was good. One of the greatest events in my life was when I found myself surrounded by two tribes of my enemies. This fight was by the El Paso River, and the bands of our enemies wore yellow headgear; the fight continued all day long until about five o'clock, when the Apaches were victorious."

By long and stubborn tutelage both from his father and the members of his tribe, this boy was taught the war spirit and in manhood he exemplified it. The principles of peace taught him in one short hour at Washington changed the whole tenor of his life: a pathetic commentary on what civilization might have accomplished with the Indian.

Climbing the Great Divide

Chief Running Bird

Chief Running Bird

Ta-ne-haddle, Chief Running Bird, is an eminent leader of the Kiowa tribe now located in Oklahoma. His massive frame, lion-like head, and dignified bearing show few of the marks of the more than threescore years written upon his life. His very walk betokens supremacy and his constant demeanour assumes a spirit of generalship. His large head is set directly upon his shoulders, which seems to give no neck-play for his voice, which issues in harsh and guttural tones.

"In the old times when the Indians used to live in tepees like this," he said, "when I was about eighteen years old, I began to go out with war parties. I have been in many wars, and lived in tents and tepees and moved from one place to another, and all this time I kept in good health. I remember a fight we had where there were thirty-eight Indians against four tribes. The battle began late in the evening and while the fight was raging high I thought I would never escape with my life. The enemy pressed us hotly, and finally we killed one of the chiefs, and then the Indians turned and left, and that saved our lives."

The construction of our Indian camp on the banks of the Little Horn awakened in this man, as it did in all the Indians, a disposition to turn back to primitive conditions. Running Bird said: "I was very glad to come here and see the old-time tepees, the kind of tepees our fathers used to live in. I grew up to manhood myself in this kind of a tepee, and I had good health, and now when they give us a house to live in I am not healthy at all. The reason we cannot have good health in a house is because the Great Father gave us tepees to live in where we have plenty of air; we feel smothered in a house. When I came out and sleep in a tepee I can sleep a great deal better. I am getting old now, and am getting up in years, and all I wish at the present time is for my children to grow up industrious and work, because they cannot get honour in the war as I used to get it. They can only get honour by working hard. I cannot teach my children the way my father taught me, that the way to get honour was to go to war, but I can teach my children that the way to get honour is to go to work and be good men and women. I shall go home and tell the other Indians and our agent about you."

And thus out of his gruff, austere, and soldier-like personality there issued words of a plain, homely philosophy that marks the path of success for all men. "The way to get honour is to go to work and be good men and women."

Chiefs Fording the Little Bighorn

Chief Brave Bear

Chief Brave Bear

Brave Bear, in the language of the Cheyennes, of whom he is head chief, is Ni-go High-ez, Ni-go meaning bear, and High-ez, brave. This name he has kept to the standard on many a hard-fought field, and in helping to reconstruct his tribe in the ways of civilization. He is tactful and courteous, and his smile resembles the sunlight breaking a path across a darkened sheet of water; it is the most winsome that I have seen for years on the face of any man.

Showing the Indian's long continued aversion to any speech regarding the Custer battle, Brave Bear said: "I was in the battle of the Little Big Horn. The Indians called the General 'Long Hair.' It is a fight that I do not like to talk about."

Just here it may be well to carry in our minds the distinction between the Northern and Southern Cheyennes. When the tribe was a compact whole they were constantly pressed farther into the plains by the hostile Sioux and established themselves on the upper branches of the Platte River. In consequence of the building of Bent's Ford upon the upper Arkansas in Colorado, a large part of the tribe decided to move south, the other section moving north to the Yellow-stone. The two sections of the one tribe have since been known officially as the Northern and Southern Cheyennes. Ever and again the Southern branch of the tribe came to the far north to help their brothers when in conflict. This may account for Brave Bear being present with the Northern Cheyennes in the Custer fight. Then came the story of Brave Bear concerning one of the battles in the south. "There is," he said, "a Cheyenne called 'Tall Bear'; he was the head man at the time we began to fight down on the Platte River. From that hard battle we were returning home. In front of us there were a lot of soldiers camped, and some of the Pawnee scouts were with the soldiers. We thought they were Pawnee tents, but when we came close enough we saw it was a soldier camp, and they fired upon us and pursued us. That day we kept on fighting, and they killed three of us. It was a great fight, and it still remains with me when I think about it."

"I like the white man's way of living to-day better, because I feel that when the new day comes everything else is new, and the things of the white man grow new with every day. I try to do as our agent directs. I have never had any trouble with him."

There is a touch of humanness about these tall, graceful, feather-bedecked men, willingly assuming the role of children, that they may learn the better ways of the white man. The hard ideals of the warpath are all merged in pursuing the path of peace.

Skirting the Sky-Line

Chief Umapine

Chief Umapine

This eminent chief of the Cayuse tribe of Umatilla Indians, located in northern Oregon, resembles in stature the graceful outlines of a forest pine. A commanding figure, six feet two inches in height, noble and dignified in bearing, quiet and reserved in manner, he creates an atmosphere of intellectuality. His speech is sparkling and eloquent. His face wears the soul-mark of serenity and triumph. As he stood against the living green of the forest, clad in the rich Indian raiment of his tribe, wolfskin, gray with the tinge of the prairies, otterskin, smooth and dark like the velvet of moss, myriads of ermine tails glistening white in the sunlight, glimmering beads from necklace to moccasins, flaunting eagle feathers tipped with orange and crimson tassels, that must have floated in many a sky, all gave to this man the appearance of some god of the forest who had just come forth from its primeval depths bringing with him the laurels of wood and mountain crag and sky, some king standing on the edge of the wood amazed at the flatness and tameness of the valley and plains. Umapine stood there the embodiment and glorification of Indian manners, costume, and tradition, a vivid picture of Indian life and story. The waymarks of such a life are, always tense with interest: they are more so as he points them out himself. We will let him tell his own story:

"It was the custom among my people to narrate to their children the history of the past and they narrated to me that my tribe had learned to make clothing from furs which were gotten from animals, and this clothing was comfortable during the winter time as well as in the summer time. There is still some of this clothing remaining among older Indians of my tribe. My understanding is that all the Indians in this part of the country used animal furs and skins for clothing. The old Indians believed in those days that they had the best kind of clothing, but they do not feel that it would be right at the present time to dress that way, as the Indians of to-day are more civilized. Yet the clothes that we have now are derived from animals. We get fur from animals, and our blankets and clothes are made from animals. From that point I cannot say which I like the better. I like the clothing of civilized people as far as I can see. The white man's clothing is fit for men to wear. I like to wear his clothes very well, but I also like to wear the clothing my people used to wear in the olden time, but I do not like to wear it now on account of my friends the white people, who live with me. I remember when I was a small boy I used to see so many wagon trains going west. I knew these were white people, but at that time I did not know where they were going. I saw these wagons going through nearly the whole summer, and my folks told me these people were going west and were to live there, and that I must not injure them in any way, and that I must have respect for them, because they were always kind to my folks. And I was instructed later to respect these people, and so I did. Furthermore, my grandfather lived on a river called Walla Walla. Many white people came to that place and put up their tents and lived there, and also there was some kind of other people which we have found were French. My grandfather had a great respect for these white people as well as his own tribe, and thought very much of them and tried to help them get along. As soon as the other tribes learned there were some white people living near my grandfather's place, there was a great gathering of the tribes to meet these white folks who were living on the river. I have it in my heart to always remember what my folks told me, and when I grew old enough to know I had respect for these white people as well as my own tribe, and to-day my heart is just the same as it was in those days.

Furthermore, I have respect for any kind of people; it does not make any difference to me from what part of the country they come. It does not make any difference whether I don't understand their language, but I always have respect for any kind of people who come to this land, and to-day I am sitting here in a strange country and I am worrying about my property in my own country, but at the same time I am rejoicing in the work that Mr. Dixon is doing here, and I highly congratulate him in this work. The work he is doing here to-day is work that may never be done any more after this, and I have a great respect for him this day because he is taking these photographs of my friends whom I meet here at this place, and whom I will never see any more. I rejoice to meet my own class of people who are coming here now. They all come from different parts of the United States. I cannot speak their language nor can I understand them all, but I do all I can to talk with them; and you, too, Mr. Valentine, I am thinking of you as I am here talking with Mr. Dixon, and at the same time I am rejoicing just as he has opened my eyes and I hope that we will get along well. I am going to say I have respect for the people you send to this country. I see that they have two eyes, they have two ears, two limbs, two feet, and fingers as I have, but we all have one head and one heart; we all breathe the same air and we stand on the earth as brothers. The only difference between myself and the white man is that his complexion is lighter than mine."

"I have a great love for you, President Taft, although I never saw your face, or never listened to any of your talk, but I know what you want, and I find you are greatly interested in the Indian, and so I am sitting here and giving the history of the Indian life, which will be a great benefit to you, and also benefit the people who are coming in later years. This evening I am rejoicing here, and I feel just as if you were present with this gentleman, and I feel just as if I were about to talk with you."

Down the Western Slope

We may pass on now to some events in the life of Umapine. Again he must speak for himself: "When I grew old enough to know something, I saw my folks digging potatoes and onions, and gathering corn; these they got from the white people the summer before. The Indians used to plant these every year, and when the emigrants went through and asked for a little my folks used to give them all they could spare. There came a time when the Indians and the white people had a war. I did not feel like interfering or trying to make any trouble, so I did not go to the war at that time. Some years after that the Indians had a fight among themselves, and I participated in that war. The Sioux Indians used to ride all over this country, and they stole horses from my tribe. When my people learned that their horses were stolen, they started on the warpath. We overtook the Sioux with the horses along about 3 P.M. as near as I can remember; we did not have watches in those days, and I think it was about that time. We killed four of the Sioux Indians and recovered our horses, the Sioux only killing one Nez Perce who was with us. I remember another war that happened not very long ago. These were Indians from the southern part of Oregon. They were on the warpath and had started up north and killed many sheep herders and farmers, and killed their children and destroyed their houses—burned them up. They came to our country and began to burn up the houses of the white farmers. These Indians came into our agency. Major Conyer, Uncle Sam's man, was agent at that time. I think he died last April. The Indians then met Uncle Sam's men about a mile and a half south of the agency, and we Indians were watching to see if the soldiers would be driven back by these Indians; we were ready to help Uncle Sam's men. The hostile Indians headed down to our camp, and when we saw them coming toward our camp we at once knew that they wanted us to get into the mixup so that we would be on the warpath as well as themselves, but all of our men got their weapons and we met these Bannock Indians and chased them back to the hills. At that time there were a few cavalrymen and the rest was infantry. All the Indians were on horseback, and the infantry could not very well keep up. We took after these Indians, but did not kill many of them, as most of them had a good start. The same evening we were requested to go with Uncle Sam's men that we might overtake these Indians and capture them if possible. The next morning we found that we were in advance of the enemy, and just as the sun rose two Indians on horseback came direct to where we were. We immediately got our arms ready and met these two Indians; one of them got so excited that he jumped off his horse and started to run for the timber, leaving his horse behind him. As he took to the thick brush we fired at him. I had a fast horse and was close behind him. I jumped off my horse and ran after him on foot. I found him lying wounded, and watched him a little while and he died. He had a very nice belt which I took and put around my waist. Meanwhile the rest of the people had the other Indian captured; he had been also wounded. Later on we saw a band of these Indians coming up direct to where we were. They had their pack animals with them. We took after them and tried to capture every one of them, but they had already seen us, and rode away for a canyon, where there was some thick brush. I saw one old woman—I thought she was an old woman—but I was mistaken, for when I overtook the Indian a man jumped off his horse and got behind a tree. When I saw my mistake, it was too late to stop my horse. I was but a few feet away from him at that time. He shot at me once and missed me. I was lucky that time or I would not be telling this story now, if he had been a better shot than that. My horse gave a big jump just as he fired at me and I kept on going, as I knew there were some more Indians close behind me who would capture the old man, and I went on after the rest of the Indians. Just as I came to a little opening I saw two Indians on horseback, and one Indian lying down on the ground; he was wounded. When I got there I learned that this Indian was a good friend of ours. I just left him there wounded. After we left I told the other two Indians: 'This man has been on the warpath, and if he had a chance to kill us he would.' So I turned back and finished his life and scalped him. My tribe captured many of those people, and I was presented with a fine animal that one of the hostile Indians had been riding. That was the only time I ever scouted for Uncle Sam".

With sublime pathos, Umapine referred to the old days of the buffalo. He said: "I have hunted buffalo in this country many times. I feel lonesome since the buffalo have been driven away. In the old days the Indians killed the buffalo with bows and arrows; they did not have any guns as they have now, and needed a fast horse to overtake these animals. A man might think they could not run fast, but he would find out he could not overtake them with an ordinary horse. My people used to hunt buffalo in this part of the country, and while on the way over here I could see trails of these large animals now worn deep by the storms of many years, and I cried in my heart."

The Last Arrow

Chief Tin-Tin-Meet-Sa

Chief Tin-Tin-Meet-Sa

It was midnight. A dim campfire accentuated the loneliness. Flickering shadows wrote weird lines on the cone-shaped walls of the tepee. The rain ceased not the beating of its soft tattoo on the frail roof above our heads. Old Tin-Tin-Meet-Sa, bent and tottering with his more than eighty years of life, his noble old face still wearing great dignity, his almost sightless eyes looking for the last flicker of life's sunset, presented a pathetic picture as he faced the firelight and told of his loneliness as he passed the deserted buffalo trails.

Tin-Tin-Meet-Sa, or Willouskin, is one of the notable chiefs of the Umatillas. He rendered valuable services to the Government as a scout during the Indian wars of 1855 and 1856. The heroic deeds of those faraway days have not been written down in history, and no doubt will be forgotten by future generations, but they have been written large on the character lines of this gigantic frame and Savonarola-like face—a poet, a dreamer, a warrior, and chieftain.

It is better to let Tin-Tin-Meet-Sa open the door himself upon that mighty past: "My days have been spent for many suns along the great rivers and high mountains of Oregon. It has been many years ago that I was selected by our agent as the head man of my tribe. In those days I was a very active man, but since I have become so old, although they look upon me as the head man of the tribe, I must leave the work for others to do. During my younger days I had a big herd of cattle and horses, but as the years have come over me, I am not able to look after my stock any more. I consider the greatest event in my life the assistance I rendered in the capture and killing of Chief Eagan, war chief of the Piutes, during the Bannock or Sheep-Eater war. These Bannock Indians created great destruction wherever they went; they burned my tepee and killed over seventy head of my cattle. I did not know at that time how many cattle I had, because there was not any one around to steal them. This led me to go on the warpath against the Bannocks."

"This country all looks familiar to me because, in my younger days, I travelled all over these prairies fighting the Sioux Indians who had stolen horses from my tribe. Again I have travelled all over this country many times, long years ago, as we came here to hunt the buffalo. I had a number of fast horses, with which I could easily kill as many buffalo as I wanted, but I only killed as many as I needed to last for a few days. When I came here the other day to meet all these chiefs, and I looked at this country for the last time, I felt lonesome when I saw how it was all changed, and all of the buffalo gone out of the country, for I could still see traces of these large animals. It is easy for an old hunter to discover these buffalo trails, for they all walked in the same place, and now the rains of many moons have cut those trails deep, just as if a man had been irrigating some field. I can scarcely see, but my eyes could find the old trail. The buffalo has gone, and I am soon going."

Chief Runs the Enemy

Chief Runs-the-Enemy

Imagine a Roman warrior with clear-cut visage and flashing eye, his face written all over with battle lines, his voice running the entire gamut from rage to mirth, and you have a mental picture of Chief Runs-the-Enemy, a tall, wiry Teton Sioux whose more than sixty-four years of life have crossed many a battlefield and won many a triumph. From boyhood days a ringing challenge to battle seemed ever vibrant in the air he breathed. When I asked him to let me drink at some of the secret springs of his life his very first sentence contained the ring of battle!

"The first thing that I remember is that my father made me a bow and arrow; it was a small bow and arrow, and made in proportion to my size, compared with the bows and arrows used in killing buffalo. I had seen the buffalo meat that they brought in and the wild game. My father taught me how to use the bow and arrow, and also how to ride a horse, and soon it became natural for me to ride. I soon grew to be able to use the bow and arrow that my father used; with it I killed buffalo. My father also taught me how to skin the buffalo, so that when I killed the buffalo I knew how to skin it and bring the buffalo meat home. My father taught me to pity the old men and women, and when I went on the warpath to be brave, and even try to die on the field. My father also taught me that it was better to go on the field of battle and have my body filled with arrows from the enemy and die on the field, and let the wolves come and eat up my flesh and bones, rather than be wrapped up and buried in some high tree, and in this spirit I went forth into all my fights. I remember when I was very young I went on the warpath and carried the bundles of moccasins and provisions for the war party. When I was fifteen years old I went with my first war party. The snow was very deep and hard, so that the horses slipped round. We charged upon the Assinaboines. I remember when we charged the camp we found one Indian down in the creek trapping foxes. We did not know he was there. As soon as he saw us he ran toward his own camp, and I whipped up my horse and ran after him. The enemy came out with guns and bows and arrows. I ran the man clear into the midst of the smoke; I came back without even myself or my horse getting hurt. That is how I got my name, Runs-the-Enemy. I was then at the age of fifteen. When we got back to camp the Sioux people said I did not know what I was doing, and I replied that I knew that was what my father had taught me. I performed this deed in the face of a lot of brave warriors, and this is how my name is great among the Sioux. There was a lifelong enmity between the Sioux and the Assinaboines. My father was wounded by the Assinaboines, and I made up my mind I was going to do something to that tribe. I have been in about forty battles altogether, rather insignificant some of them, but about ten great battles. When I was about eighteen, a band of Sioux, including myself, went down to the Black Rees. They greatly outnumbered us. We attacked them, but did not kill any of them. They pursued us a long way, killing five of our number. My horse was hit with an arrow, and I jumped off, and while I was running I was shot through the ankle with an arrow. The enemy surrounded me; my own friends had gone on. I crossed my wounded ankle over the other foot and defended myself as best I could. I looked at the ground and the sky, and made up my mind that this was my last day. Just at this moment, while I was surrounded by my enemies, one of my friends was brave enough to come back; he rode into the midst of our foes and put me on the back of his horse, and we rode away in safety. Let me tell you about the other wound that I received. In one of the late battles that we had with the tribe of Black Rees, in 1874, I was shot through the thigh, a ball also going through the forearm, and breaking the bone."

Scouting Party on the Plains

"Let me tell you about my connection with the battle of the Little Rosebud. With my war party I joined the Sioux camp on the Rosebud River. We camped first at Lame Deer. When I arrived at the Sioux camp at Lame Deer we were near the Cheyenne camp, and the Cheyennes had built a big bonfire. They were singing and dancing around the fire. I was told that there were some Cheyennes that had reached camp that day or the day before from the Black Hills, and they brought the news that the soldiers were coming. The reason for the campfire and the dancing was to pick out the bravest of the Cheyennes and send them back to find out the location of the troops and bring back word. The campfire was so big and so bright and the dancing and shooting so boisterous that I went over to the Cheyenne camp to see for myself. And I saw them choosing the braves for this scouting duty. The scouts must have numbered ten. They started right off on their mission. The next morning we broke camp and came over the hills. We camped about half a day's journey from the Custer battlefield. That night, after we camped, there was no news, and I went to bed and went to sleep. The next morning I was awakened by firing, and the report came to me that there was going to be trouble, for the troops were coming. Almost at once everybody who could ride a horse or hold a gun mounted his horse and rode away to meet the troops. The Cheyenne scouts led the way. It was not very long until I heard the report of rifles, over in the gully. After the report of the guns we heard a cry from the hilltop; an Indian was on the hill crying as hard as he could, telling us to make the charge at once. Then one of their number was killed outright. The occasion of the shots was that four or five of our Sioux had gone around us and had gone into the soldiers' camp and stolen some horses, and the soldiers were firing at the horse-thieves; four of them escaped, one being killed. This was the screaming we heard. We no sooner heard it than we made a dash. I cannot tell you the number of our Indians. There were the different bands of the Sioux, and the entire tribe of the Cheyennes. The charge we made was enough to scare anybody. As we got on top of the hill the soldiers, who were already after the horse-thieves, knowing that we outnumbered them, all fled back. The cavalry supported by a file of infantry stopped, and we also stopped and had a great battle there. We simply circled them, and did not give them a chance to charge, as we greatly outnumbered them. We killed a great many soldiers, shot down a good many of their horses, for there were lots of them lying on the ground, wounded and dead. This battle the Indians called the Battle of the Wolf Mountains, known to the soldiers and the Crows by this name, and to the Sioux as the Battle of the Head of the Rosebud. The general sentiment was that we were victorious in that battle, for the soldiers did not come upon us, but retreated back into Wyoming. We understood that General Crook was in command of the United States troops, led by Crow scouts. They called General Crook, 'Three Stars.' When our Indians made the charge upon the United States troops we found the Crow scouts standing between us and the troops. If it had not been for the Crow scouts we would have charged right through to the soldiers. The Crow scouts were in between us, and received the fire from both sides. After the battle ended and the soldiers returned, we got home to our camp without any fear. We spent the whole of the next day in camp at the Little Rosebud, and the day after we came over on to the plains by the Custer Battlefield."

Scouts passing under cover of the Night

The most graphic Indian story of the Custer fight is told by Runs-the-Enemy in the chapter on "The Indians' Story of the Custer Fight." Chief Runs-the-Enemy continued:

"A great event in changing my life was marked when I returned to the reservation and the Government took from us our horses and guns and told us that we were to live in that place at peace with everybody. The Government took the best warriors from among the tribe, made them lift their hands to God and swear that they would be true to the Government; and they made out of these men policemen who were to guard the Government and keep the Indians good. When the Government made a policeman of me they bound my hands with chains and I had to obey them. They gave me implements with which to till the soil, and raise stock and build a home, and it seemed to me I must obey every word they said. They told me that the wild game, now roaming the hills, would soon die off, and that if I tilled the soil and raised stock and grain, I could get money for it, and money is what makes everything move along. As I told you, whatever they told me, I did. They told me to send my children to school, which I did. I sent all of my children to school, and they came home and all of them died. They told me if I sent the children to school and educated them, they would be all right. Instead of that I sent them to school and they all came home with consumption and died, seven in number. If I had kept them home, some of them might have been living to-day. Now as to myself: I am getting old every day; I cannot take care of my stock. My limbs are weak, and my knees are getting weak; it will not be long until I will go under the ground. As you look at me now I am old. As I said, I will die in a little while, but I am not afraid of dying. I have two children living and I look ahead for them. Although I have done all I could for my people, I have also helped the Government and done whatever they told me to do."

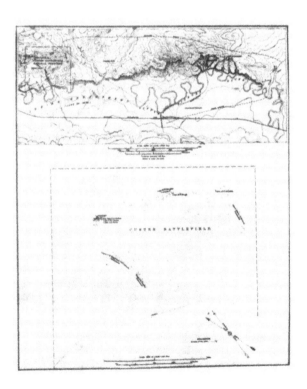

Map of the Custer Battlefield

We have been listening to the minor in the carol, that is always the major strain in Indian life, but we mistake much if we do not hear more jubilant notes in the scale. When Runs-the-Enemy was asked to tell the story of his boyhood days all the fierce combativeness expressed in gesture, voice, and piercing eye gave way to a tender and gentle calm. The warrior became a child, living again the life of a child with all the spontaneous gleefulness of a child. We may now have one of his folklore tales.

FOLKLORE TALE

There goes a spider. As he was journeying along he came upon a man—in our legends these men do anything; they take a whole community of men right down—and he met him face to face. The man-eater stood in the path, the spider in front of him. The big man kept letting out his breath and taking it in in great gusts, and when he drew in his breath he drew the spider toward him, and when he blew out his breath he blew him away from him. And the spider was so scared he did not know what to do. But he finally said: "Now, my young brother, you take in your breath, and let out your breath, and you pull me around; and if I did the same thing you would soon be gone, for I am older than you are." The big man said to the spider: "Now, my older brother, you hold on." The spider said to the big man: "I am going over here where there is a great big camp of people, and I am going to swallow all of these people. However, as you are hungry, I will give you half of them. Now you stay right here. I am going over to look at the big camp. I am going to find out whether I will give you any of them or not, and then I will tell you." With these words the spider went ahead of the man a little, and then came right back to the big man again and said: "My young brother, I am afraid of some certain things, and I am going to tell you about it. Are you the same way?" The big man said: "Yes, my little brother, I am very much afraid of some things." The spider then asked him: "What are the things you are afraid of?" The big man then told the spider that he was afraid of drums beating, that he was afraid of old tambourines that the Indians used to have, and he was also afraid of shouting and yelling. The spider then said to him: "You are my brother for sure; these are just the things that I am afraid of." Just as he said these things to the big man, the spider was very much afraid of him, fearing that he could not hold himself steady as he stood in front of the big man. The spider said to the big man: "You just sit right still here. I am going over to see this big camp, and will be right back." The spider went over the hill as fast as he could, looking back every once in a while to the big man. He went right ahead into the big camp. He told everybody around there to get all their drums and their tambourines, that he had a great big man over there, and these were the things that he was afraid of. "I am going back to him and

I want you to take all your drums and tambourines, and yell and scream, for he is afraid of these things." The spider then went back to the big man and told him the camp was big enough for them both. Then he marked a place which divided them half and half, and said: "You are to have the one half and I am to have the other half; but if you go ahead and eat your half and eat half of my half, I will swallow you too." As they went along to the camp the spider said to the big man: "I am the older, and will go ahead of you a little." In the meantime he had told those in camp that they must all gather in one place where he would lead this big man. As the big man walked along, he grew tired, and would let out his breath and take in a great big breath, and every time the spider would be drawn up against him. The spider told him if he did it again he would draw in his breath and the big man would soon be inside his stomach. As the spider went on into the place where all the people were gathered, they began to beat their drums and yell and scream and howl. The spider fell down as though he were dead, and kicked and squirmed. The big man was really scared, and he fell down dead. When they got up to the big man and found him dead, the spider told them how he had worked the big man, and saved their lives. And thus the story ends.

Chief Pretty Voice Eagle

Chief Pretty Voice Eagle

Sixty-eight years is a long time to be an Indian. Within this span of life Pretty Voice Eagle has run with swift feet the warpath, and held with strong hand the battle spear. Bearing well his weight of years and his heavier burden of struggle, he moves erect and with lithe footstep. He became stormy and vociferous as he told his story of broken treaties, how the Indian had been wronged by the white man, and how his life had been scarred by the storms of life. Then the calm of old age came over him and the placid joy of childhood memories when asked to tell a folklore tale. While relating his battle experiences we had the equinoctial gale of Indian life and then the mellow haze of Indian summer. Recalling his boyhood days, Pretty Voice Eagle told me that his tribe roamed along the river, chiefly the Missouri River. There were then no white people in that country. "I was about ten years old when I saw large boats bringing white people over the Missouri River. I saw a great many of the white people killed by the Sioux when they came up the river in small boats. It was not until I was about twenty years old that they began to build the railroad along the Platte River going west, and there were also emigrant wagons going west driving large herds of cattle. The Indians killed the white people as they came up the river because we felt they were driving away our game; they had guns and powder and knives, which we did not have. We also wanted what they had in the boats, and we did not like to see them go through our country. When I first saw the people emigrating through our country and then bringing iron horses there I began to be afraid. I was about twenty-five or thirty years old when they began to run the iron horse along through the country, and I also heard that they were going to move the Indians to some hot country, and that the white people would fill up all the land north and west and south of us; we felt that we ought to fight the white people, and we began to kill the men who were building the railroad. The white people began to kill the game when they came into the country. There was then plenty of buffalo on the east side of the Missouri River; soon they swam over to the west side, and we then understood that the President had given them the privilege of killing all the game, and soon the buffalo were all gone. The white man then went into the Black Hills, and killed the game. The killing of the game caused a change in our food. We were accustomed to eating buffalo meat and other wild game; we loved that and we were all full of health as long as we had it. The change of food has compelled us to eat bread instead of wild meat, and that is the reason why the Indians are all dying off. When I think of those old days my heart is full of sorrow. My father, who was then the chief, was sent for by the President of the United States, and when he came back he said that the Indians must adopt the white man's mode of living, and that we must send our children to school. The news that my father brought was received by some with favour, others entirely refused to send their children to school, and said that they would rather fight than let their children go to school. And it looked as though there would be a general uprising. I remember the first group who went off to school, and it caused great trouble. From that time on we had trouble with the United States soldiers. While we were carrying this trouble about the schools in our minds, there was an emigrant train going through the Black Hills. They had with them a cow which was lame, and and they left it. The Indians thought they had thrown it away, and killed it. We killed this cow not for subsistence but because it was lame and we felt sorry for it. It was not until a year later that the people who owned this cow made application to the Government for reimbursement for the loss, and the

Government sent United States soldiers there to find out who had killed the cow. The two men who had killed the cow were Face Powder and Pointed Forehead. They asked us to give up these men that they might take them to Fort Laramie, and we refused to give them up. They then asked our head chief, Axe-the-Bear, to give them up, and when he would not do so he was taken to Fort Laramie. Part of the Sioux Nation was at Fort Laramie, and they wanted to know why the soldiers had taken this head chief there. It was a mistake of the interpreter, for he told the officers in command that the Sioux Indians were there to kill the soldiers if they did not give up this head chief. One of the soldiers rather than let the chief go ran him through with a bayonet and killed him in cold blood. As soon as they killed this chief, the Indians began to fight right there. There was a running fight after that until they finally captured Spotted-Tail with his band and squaws and children. A lot of Spotted-Tail's men were killed. They afterward gave up the women and children. That did not satisfy the Indians; they wanted revenge on the soldiers and had a battle west of the Black Hills. After that big battle the Indians were chased right into the territory where the present camp of the great chiefs is located. Following that there was another big battle on the east side of the Missouri River. The women and children were all captured. Following this there was a treaty with the United States not to fight. The treaty was signed up near Fort Laramie. The trouble still kept up, the treaty was broken, and we had another big battle near the Rocky Mountains, where a hundred soldiers were killed. After that there were several battles, including the Custer fight, and then the bands all split up, some of them going to Canada and some of them back to the reservations where they are now located. Then there was a delegation sent to Washington, and when they came back to the people from the Indian Department, we sent our children to school. The Indians who went to Canada afterward returned. A great many Sioux remained on the reservation at the time of the Custer fight; I was not in the battle myself. I saw General Custer when he left Fort Lincoln previous to the Custer fight. Custer impressed me as a very pleasant and good man; he wore his hair long. As he was about to leave Fort Lincoln a delegation of Sioux Indians, including myself, went to see him and asked him not to fight the Sioux Indians, but to go to them in a friendly way. I was the leader of the delegation. We begged him to promise us that he would not fight the Sioux. He promised us, and we asked him to raise his hand to God that he would not fight the Sioux, and he raised his hand. After he raised his hand to God that he would not fight the Sioux he asked me to go west with my delegation to see those roaming Sioux, and tell them to come back to the reservation, that he would give them food, horses, and clothing. After we got through talking, he soon left the agency, and we soon heard that he was fighting the Indians and that he and all his men were killed. If Custer had given us time we would have gone out ahead of him, but he did not give us time. If we had gone out ahead of Custer he would not have lost himself nor would his men have been killed. I did all I could to persuade the Ree scouts not to go with Custer. I gave them horses and saddles not to go, but for some reason they went."

A War Council

"In the treaty the Government made with me at Fort Laramie, they were to feed me fifty-five years, and they have not fulfilled it. You must be a man of influence, as you sent for us from all parts of the country, and I wish you would help us as much as you can. In the Fort Rice treaty the Government promised to give us good horses and good wagons."

"After the 1868 treaty that we had at Fort Rice we sold all the country east of the Missouri River and soon sold the Black Hills to the Government, and in that treaty the Government promised us that the Sioux Indians would be taken care of as long as there was a child living of the Sioux tribe; and that has not been fulfilled. It was not long after that when we had a treaty with General Crook. In that treaty we were promised a great many things the Government did not seem to care to do. Now our funds are almost exhausted, and a lot of us are poor and not able to take care of ourselves, and I wish that when you go back you would say what you can. These are Government promises, and they have never fulfilled them."

"The story I am going to tell you I am not afraid to have published anywhere, or to have it come right back to my own agency, or let other warriors see and hear it. In my lifetime I have made about seventy raids against the different tribes. Out of these raids there must have been forty-five or fifty battles. Let me tell you a story concerning one of these battles in which I was engaged: I was a young man, I cannot remember just what age. The Sioux camped at the mouth of the Rosebud River. We got up a war party which numbered about two hundred. The two bands who were in this party were the Two-Cattle and the Mnik-Ok-Ju tribes. It was in the middle of the winter when the snow was deep. We started across the country not very far from this camp, and followed the Yellowstone River down, and then we turned off toward the north, and went toward the Upper Rockies. We were then in the enemy's country. There were four of us chosen out of the two bands to go ahead and scout for the enemy; we did not see any one, and returned. There was one man from our party out shooting deer, and he was right behind us. We got home without seeing anything, but he brought word there were enemies in sight. The enemies he saw were two in number, and we got on our horses and went to where he saw these two men. They were well armed and did all they could to defend themselves, and our party did not come very close to them. I spurred up my horse and made a straight charge at the two men. They were on foot, and lined up and pointed their guns at me as I went at them. I struck one of them with the spear that I had. I knocked him down; he fired at me, but missed me. The other man also fired at me, but missed. I could not strike him, as I dodged after I struck the first man. As I passed on by them they fired at me again. This gave my warriors a chance to come up on them before they could reload their guns, and they killed them. I was the first one who struck one and very nearly hit the other. My warriors were slow to come up, and I was the first one to charge them. After we killed these two men we went home with their scalps. We were on our way home across the Powder River and following the river up until we got to the junction of the Powder and Rosebud rivers. When we got there one of our party went on home ahead of us. He came rushing toward us with his horse almost played out, with the report that the camp had been attacked by the enemy while we were away, and they had stolen our horses, and were now coming down the road on which we were travelling. We hid waiting for them, but somehow they became aware of our presence, and went around, and before we knew it they had escaped. Although they were a great ways off our band made a charge on these horsemen. Most of our horses gave out before we overtook the enemy, but thirteen of us rode on, overtaking them, three in number we found, who had charge of the stolen horses. Our thirteen horses that we were riding were nearly exhausted, but we found that the enemy whom we were pursuing were also riding exhausted horses. I rushed on ahead as fast as my horse could go. One of the enemy was riding a horse that was so thoroughly given out that he stood still. The enemy got off his horse, turned round, pulled his bow and arrow, and shot at me; I was going to strike him, but I did not have time. The arrow was so near my face that it made me dizzy. He fired at me and the arrow went right through my hair, which was tied in a knot on top of my head. I jumped off my horse and pulled my bow and arrow, and we were firing at each other as we came closer. We jumped round like jack-rabbits trying to dodge the arrows. One of the arrows struck me right across the ribs, but the wound was not very deep. Just as we came together he fired his last arrow at me; it passed through my arm, but it was only a skin wound. At that time I struck him with my arrow through the wrist and that made him lame. As I struck him he moved backward and I shot him twice through the breast, with two arrows; then I threw away the arrows and struck him on the head with my bow, knocking him senseless. After I knocked him down I took his bow and threw it a long ways off so he could not get it. He was crawling on his hands and knees and I took my war club and struck him until I killed him. After I had killed this man, I gathered up my bow and arrows, and went on after the other two. At this time they had got off their horses and were defending themselves as best they could. I shot one of them through the wrist with my arrow; he made a scream as I hit him and dodged and went down the coulee, running as hard as he could go. He had a revolver in one hand, and I followed him, shooting with my arrows, he shooting back at me with his revolver. This kept up until he got to the end of the coulee, where there was a deep precipice. I looked over the precipice and saw this man, who had jumped over, rolling down the side like a rock. When he got down there he was knocked senseless. I looked at him from over the hill, but could not get down to him. I walked back and forth; as I looked down I saw a Sioux Indian trying to crawl up and get the scalp of the Indian who had fallen down the precipice. I had a war club in my teeth, and grabbed my bow and arrows, and tried to climb down the hill slope in order that I might get near him. As I went down I slid, and as I was going down the Crow regained consciousness and I saw him pointing his gun at me as I was looking down. I then thought that would be my last day. As I got there the Sioux got there just in time to grab the revolver away from him, and as he pulled the revolver away I fell right under the enemy. He pulled a knife out of my belt, for I was under him, pushed up against a rock, and I could not move either way. He made a strike at me and cut my clothing right across the abdomen, but did not cut my stomach. The second strike he made, I got hold of the knife, and wrested it from him. When I had taken the knife, the other Sioux pulled him off, and I got up and took my club and finished him. I killed these two Crows a little ways from the mouth of the Little Big Horn that flows through the camp where we are now. This is one of the daring events of my life. These two events occurred in one war party."

The War Party

"Then, again, let me tell you about the battle that we had between the Sioux and the Flatheads about twenty miles north of where Billings now stands: In this battle the Sioux numbered about one hundred and fifty, and the Flatheads consisted of the entire tribe. We sent three spies across the Yellowstone, and they came back with the location of the Flatheads. They reported that the entire tribe was camped there. We were afraid because of their great numbers that they would beat us. We debated as to whether we should go back home or make the attack. Finally the chiefs selected thirty of the bravest men to go on ahead. The rest of the war party remained in camp. I was numbered among the thirty who were chosen to go ahead. We left there in the dark of the night. We journeyed on in silence until daybreak, when we first got a view of the enemy's camp. When daylight came we found that ten of our thirty had deserted from fear. When we got in sight of the camp another ten left us, so that only left ten to advance on the camp. We made a fool charge at the camp at the rising of the sun. None of us expected to come back when we made the charge. After we made the charge, there were about four who backed out again, so that left us only six in number. We ran our horses up to the side of the tents and then ran back again to the hills. The women were just getting out to get breakfast ready. We took about fifty horses with us, as we rode back, as a challenge for the enemy to come after us. The firing began from the camp and frightened the horses so that we only got about twenty out of the fifty. There was one horse, a spotted animal, that pleased me very much, and out of the six of us in number I rushed back to get that horse. When I went back after this horse the enemy came upon me so strong that I was obliged to flee to the hills. They came right behind us firing at us. The enemy chased us for miles and miles, shooting at us but never killing any of us. We turned in our saddles every once in a while and fired back, and then went on. We were reinforced by the last ten that left us. Just at this time a horse under one of our men was shot, and he was on foot running. We made a whirl around this man who was on foot, which seemed to check the enemy. At this time one of the enemy was shot off his horse. This man who was shot from his horse was surrounded by two of his friends who dismounted to defend him. As soon as I saw this man lying on his back, I made a hard charge at him; I struck at his head. An enemy standing near discharged his gun at me, and took the butt of the gun to strike me on the head. Just at this moment my horse stumbled and fell forward which saved me from receiving the blow. As I did so I made a circle and came back again to my own people. But I was mad at him in my heart because he had struck at me. I took my bow and arrow and shot an arrow right through his cheek. As I hit this enemy through the cheek I whipped up my horse and made a charge at him. One of my friends came riding up with me, and we both charged together. Our horses turned just as we reached this enemy whom I had shot through the cheek, and the enemy ran right in behind us. He got hold of my friend's horse's tail and shot him through the back with his revolver and he fell right over my horse. I got off my horse, holding my friend tight, and one of my friends saw the enemy at this time and shot him. This man who had been shot by my friend got up again as his wound was only a skin wound. I let go of my dead friend and got off my horse and charged at this fellow. Just as I charged at him there were two angry Sioux who laid their coup sticks on him. They went on by him and that left him for me to fight. Just as I reached him the enemy was very close behind me. They had shot at me at very close range. I could smell the smoke. He aimed his gun right at me, but he was so bewildered that he did not fire. I took the gun away from him and knocked him down. I got on my horse, taking his gun with me, at which time my horse was shot across the nose, but he kept on going toward my friends. The bullets whizzed around me, bewildering me for a moment. At this time it seemed as though the enemy were defeated, but the rest of our band came up at this moment. The enemy retreated when they saw our friends, but they pursued us all the way back to the Yellowstone. The dead numbered about a hundred in this battle. I did not go back, because my horse was exhausted. I have five more just such thrilling stories, including the one in which I was wounded."

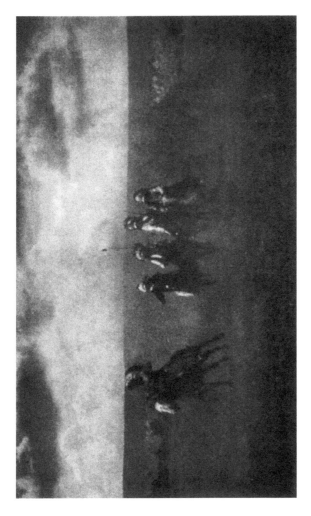

The Swirl of the Warriors

"The greatest event in my life, leaving behind the story that I have told, is to be found at the time the Indians received allotments of land, and were given a home so they could not roam around; and above all, the time when I found religion and became a Christian. I was baptized and confirmed in the Episcopal Church. I married my wife under the holy bonds of matrimony, and am trying to live an upright life. In the roaming life, I fought, I took many scalps, and killed many Indians. Now, put alongside of that the fact that I live in my own home, own my land, have my own family, and am a church member. I like the last life better than the first. In the former life while we lived to ourselves, we were always fighting; in the life now we have peace. The one thing now that is killing me off is our mode of life. There is too much confinement; instead of fighting the enemy, I am fighting disease. The white people know about everything, but if they can kill that foul disease, consumption, I shall feel very thankful. As I told you before, I think of the buffalo time, the meat, and the hides, and the desire for it seems almost like a disease, and this is especially true with the old men."

When asked about his belief concerning the Indian's hereafter, before he became a Christian, he replied: "There was no definite Supreme Being that we believed in. There were a great many gods that we had faith in. I prayed to my own god; then we all heard that after we died we would meet in some good country where we would all be happy. No matter if we had lots of gods, we would all meet in that country. Now, while I cannot read the Bible, nor can I understand the Bible, yet we have preachers in our own language and they tell us that there is one God, and also His Holy Son, and we shall all meet in heaven, and I believe in that. A great many of the Sioux are followers like I am, but like a great many other people, there are many who do one thing and feel another. In the old days the sun was my god, the sun was my fathef's god, and I then thought the sun was my father and the earth was my mother. I sang and danced to the sun; I have my breast and arms tattooed with the sun, and I pierced my body through offering sacrifices to the sun. Now I look back upon those old Indian customs as foolishness. It is like a man coming out of darkness into light. I was then in the dark; I am now going into the valley of light, learning every day."

Folklore Tales—Sioux

Pretty Voice Eagle reached the other pole of life when his thoughts went back to the time when the old folks gathered around the campfire, and as a small lad he listened to their oft-repeated stories. "I can hardly remember them, but I will tell you a short story: There was a great big spider carrying a big roll of straw on his back, and he was running along between two lakes. There was a great big flock of geese on one of the lakes. One of the geese yelled over to the spider: 'Spider, where are you going?' The spider said: 'You hush up now! I have heard there is a camp of Indians over here who have returned from a victory with many scalps, and they sent for me with my songs. I have them all in the bundle on my back, and I am taking them over to them.' The spider kept on going, and one of the geese told him: 'You stop, and give us one of those songs you are taking over there.' The spider kept on going; said he was in a terrible hurry, but he still kept making the circle of the lake; he wanted the geese to yell to him again, which they did, and finally the spider yelled over to the geese: 'If you want one of my songs, come over here.' The spider made a little booth of straw. He had a little stick and was standing in the door. When the geese came over he told them to go in the booth, and when they did so, he sang a song, and told every one to close his eyes, for every one who opened his eyes would have red eyes. Of course they all closed their eyes, and he set about knocking them all down. One of the geese happened to open his eyes, and he called out to the other geese: 'Open your eyes and fly away; this spider is going to kill you all!' and he flew away. The spider said: 'You will have red eyes forever!' And so it is that the duck called hell-diver has red eyes."

Here is another story: There was a solitary man going along, and he had a lot of meat on his back. On his journey he stopped under some trees, built a great big fire, and was broiling some of the meat that he was carrying. The branches of two trees standing near got crossed over each other and when the wind blew made a squeaking noise. The man looked up to the tree, and said: "My brothers, you quit fighting up there!" The creaking continued, and he called up to them again to stop their fighting. But it still continued, and he finally said: "I am going to part you two; you must stop fighting." And he put his hand up between the two branches; as he put his hand between them the wind stopped blowing. His hand was caught and he was not able to get away. Just then a wolf passed along, and the man saw him and called out to him: "Go on about your business, and let my things alone." The wolf did not know anything about the broiled meat being there, but when this man called to him, he said to himself: "That man must have something for me," and he walked over to the broiled beef, took it all, and went his way. After the wolf had gone the wind blew again, and the man released his hand, and the squeaking began again. The man cried, and was sorry in his heart, and began trailing the wolf by his tracks. He went on till he came to a body of water, in which he plunged. He looked down into the water, and saw the wolf eating his meat. He dove down into the water, and felt all around and was nearly exhausted when he came out. He then got up in a tree and when the water became still again, there was the wolf down in the water again, so the man got down and tied a rope around his belt, piled some rocks on his side so he could stay down there long enough to get the wolf. During all this time the wolf was on the branch of the tree above him; the reflection of the wolf was in the water. When the man got down in the water, the weight of the rocks held him there, and he began to struggle to get out, and just barely succeeded in getting out of the water. Just as he got out of the water, he looked up and saw the wolf on the top of the tree. The man's sides were so filled with stones that he had great difficulty in getting up the steep bank, so much so that he could hardly crawl to the top of the bank, and as he was struggling to get out, the wolf finished eating the meat, jumped down, and ran away. So ends the story.

The life of the Indian is complex. To gather up the sixty-eight years of this man's life means that we round out a problem of infinite dimensions. His cradle lullaby, a war song; his earliest memories, stained with the blood of the white man; his unshaken valour on the field of battle; scars left on his soul by the broken treaties of the white man; his devotion to the mysterious gods in the pantheon of Nature; his unrequited lament at the loss of the buffalo; his natural eloquence born from the throne room of Nature: his final love of peace and acceptance of the shining face of the Son of Righteousness all lay upon civilization the heavy hand of condemnation.

Chief White Horse

Chief White Horse

"My father told me I was born in the Black Hills. Ever since I can remember my people have lived on the shores of the Bad River, South Dakota. While I lived there I saw the white people for the first time coming up the river in the big boats. At this time the buffalo were on both sides of the Missouri River, and there was plenty of game and we were all living fat at that time. It was not very long before the fort was built at the mouth of the Bad River. My father liked to be with the white people, and we were up at the store a good deal. The fort finally became a great trading post. The Indians brought in skins of the various animals, such as beaver, wolf, fox, panther, and buffalo. While I was still a young boy I left that section of the country and came further west with the other Indians. I have always tried to live without making any trouble among my own people or with the whites. When I got out among the Sioux I began to learn some of their wild tricks. I began to learn to fight the other Indians. I then went on the warpath, and have been in a good many Indian fights. One fight in particular against the Assinaboines I want to mention. In this battle there were about two hundred of us Sioux. The fight was on the Missouri River. There were charges and countercharges several times. One of the bravest came in advance of the others but he had to retreat. I put two arrows in his back and then rushed up and knocked him off his horse with my bow. After I had knocked this man off his horse my own horse ran away with me and ran right into the enemy's line, dashing in among the foe. They were firing arrows at me from all sides, and I expected that this was my last day. This was the greatest fight I was ever in, though I have been in many others."

It is a long step from the spear to the ploughshare, but the moccasined feet of White Horse soon took the step. Concerning this epoch in his life, he said: "The most important event in my life was when the Government began to give annuities to the Indians and we were placed on the reservation. I have always been a leader of the Indians and a chief. When farming implements were assigned us, and the allotments made, I was appointed head farmer over the Indians. I visited the Indians all over my district, and tried to get them to till the soil and send their children to school. I sent my own boy to school first as an example to the others. I sent my children to a nearby school until they were old enough and then I was one of the first to send my children to Hampton, Virginia, to school. They all came home and died of consumption. About this time the first missionary came to our country, and I was one of the first to be converted to the Church. I have since done all I could to bring the other Indians into the Church. I went at my own expense down to the place where I now live. There were no people living there at the time, and I cut out of the woods the logs and built a church in my own home. I had no help. The Indians came there to church, and afterward they named the church the White Horse Church. After this a settlement was made here by the Indians, and finally the Government made a post-office at this place, and they called it the White Horse post-office. It has since become a sub-agency. The influence thus brought to bear on the Indians had led them to live a good deal as the white man lives. I have my farm now, raise cattle and horses. All I have done for the Government and for the Church I have been glad to do, for they have all been kind to me. While other Indians have been fighting and making trouble for the United States I have never participated in any of it."

Before passing to the folklore tale that fell from the lips of Chief White Horse, the attention of the reader is especially directed to the chapter on Indian Impressions of the last Great Council, where White Horse describes his feelings and the lessons he learned while riding for the first time on the iron horse.

Folklore Tales—Yankton Sioux

"In the evenings of my boyhood days my father always told stories. I remember that I used to go to sleep while he was telling stories. This is one of the stories he used to tell: There goes a wolf on a journey. He came upon three buffalo. The wolf said to the buffalo: 'My brothers, make me as one of you, and we will all live together.' The buffalo told him: 'Will you stand the life that we live?' The wolf said 'Yes,' and they all told him to go a distance off and lie down on his back. The buffalo was going to make the wolf a buffalo, and he lay down on his back and sides and rolled in the dust, and then he got up and shook himself and he then made a plunge for the wolf and stuck his horns in him and threw him in the air. Just as he got to the wolf, the wolf jumped aside, and the buffalo said: 'You made me make that hard run for nothing.' The wolf said: 'Try again.' The buffalo said: 'This time you stand up and I will come at you.' So the wolf stood a good ways off. Just as the buffalo reached the wolf, the wolf turned into a buffalo, and they locked horns with each other. And thus he became a strong buffalo. He roamed with the buffalo for a while. The other buffalo went off a little way by themselves and grazed on the grass while the wolf-buffalo took the first grass near where he stood. While he was eating there another wolf came along, and he said to the buffalo: 'Make me a buffalo, and we will all be brothers together.' This wolf buffalo then told the wolf to stand just as he had stood before. This wolf buffalo lay down on his back and rolled in the dust and went for the wolf, and as he was going to strike him he turned back again into a wolf, and the two wolves were there together fighting. The wolf buffalo said: 'I was happy as a buffalo, and was living fat—why did you come around here and make me into a wolf again?' And he began to fight him. And thus the story ends. And this is why the Indians are always fighting each other."

Chief Bear Ghost

Chief Bear Ghost

The great Siouan, or Dakota family, is divided into many different tribes. They are the dislocated remains of the "Seven Great Council Fires." The Indians resent the title of Sioux, meaning "Hated Foe," and prefer the word Dakota, which means "Leagued," or "Allied." There is the Brule Sioux, meaning "Burnt Hip"; the Teton, "On a Land without Trees"; the Santee Sioux, "Men Among Leaves," a forest; the Sisseton Sioux, "Men of Prairie Marsh," and the Yankton Sioux, which means, "At the End." Chief Bear Ghost is a Yankton Sioux. Among the Dakotas the chiefs are distinguished by a name that has either some reference to their abilities, having signalized themselves on the warpath or in the chase, or it may be handed down from father to son. Chief Bear Ghost bears the hereditary name of his father, Mato-wanagi—the ghost of a bear. The Dakotas count their years by winters, and all their records are called winter counts. They say a man is so many snows old, or that so many snow-seasons have occurred since a certain period. Adopting their own phrasing Chief Ghost Bear is fifty-seven snows old. Custer was not poetical when he gave the Sioux the name of "cut-throats," but he may have been true to the character and history of these fierce and warlike tribes. We may not wonder then that Bear Ghost should say: "The greatest event in my life was the participation in two great wars. I was on the warpath on the Missouri River against the Gros Ventres and the Mandans. It was a hard, fierce struggle; we had been facing and shooting each other from early dawn until the sun went down. An Indian near me, an enemy, was shot, and when I went after him my horse was shot, but still I pressed on and struck the enemy with a tomahawk. One of the enemy aimed at me, but I struck him with the tomahawk before he could shoot, and when this struggle was over the Indians called us men. In other years we came to that same place again. Two enemies were near the camp; they were armed with guns. There were seven of the enemy and but two of us. We went right up to the camp. I shot one of the enemy and wounded him, and captured one of their horses. Then a great number of Indians came out and chased us. They surrounded us, shooting all the while, and the horse I had taken from the enemy I shot rather than let them have it. And while they were chasing me my horse became exhausted and I had to get off and lead him. I ran into the creek where my enemies were on the banks shooting at me. These two things I consider the greatest events in my life, for I expected to die each time. Then I was made head chief of my tribe."

Before the police system was established on the reservation, Bear Ghost, along with one other Indian, was detailed by Captain Daugherty to watch for and capture a man who had committed murder. Bear Ghost succeeded in carrying out this commission, and the sheriff was sent for and the prisoner turned over to him, but on the way to Bismarck the prisoner killed the sheriff, jumped onto the best horse, and made his escape. Bear Ghost has often been chosen by his people to represent them at councils held among other tribes. He was also sent to Washington, on matters pertaining to treaties made years ago. He wears the countenance of a Roman senator; he is tall, graceful, and full of dignity, a forceful and convincing speaker, and a compelling advocate of peace.

Chief Running Fisher

Chief Running Fisher [2]

The story of this war-scarred Gros Ventres veteran emphasizes with double pathos the many times expressed sentiment of this book that the Indian is a vanishing race, for he died within two weeks after returning home from the last Great Indian Council. His words, therefore, are deeply significant: "I feel sad at the thought of not meeting these chiefs again, for I would like to meet them all once more, but I feel pretty sure we will never meet again."

Chief Running Fisher had measured threescore years of life, and for forty years of that time he had averaged a battle for every other year. Battles in

Canada, battles in the mountains, and battles on the plains. He had fought the Sioux, the Blackfeet, the Nez Perce, the Crows, the Shoshones, and the Piegans. He said: "I have twenty shots in my body received in battle. I have had my arm broken and wrist sprained. A bullet went right through one of my arms. In early days I fought with the bow and arrow. In one battle I killed two men, shooting a single arrow through them both. The greatest event of my life occurred when I was shot at the battle of Big Spring and left for dead on the field. My friends kept back the enemy as long as they could and when they saw that I did not revive they left me. I was bleeding from the inside, a coughing of blood out of the throat brought me to. When I came to I found the enemy had departed and I followed the tracks of my own tribe. Some of my friends were shot and I could see by the blood stains on the snow the path they had taken. I was nineteen years of age at this time. It was a long time before I overtook the band. They travelled much faster than I could, but I finally reached the camp and recovered. We had no surgeons and but little care. Every Indian had to be his own doctor. I will tell you about another close call I had. The event that I am now about to relate is the main thing that makes a chief out of a warrior. We had a fight with the Piegans. One of the Piegans had a gun and a dagger, one in each hand. This Piegan ran at me and I ran at him. As we came together I grabbed the Piegan's gun with one hand and his dagger with the other and as I warded off his charge, his gun was fired, and I took the gun and the dagger away from him. Then my friends rushed to my rescue and killed the Piegan and scalped him."

Turning from battles and wounds, let this old chieftain recur to his boyhood days: "I remember when I was quite a boy the wonderful sun dance. It greatly impressed me. I could not understand it and I asked my father about it and he told me that I could not take part in the sun dance until I had earned my title as a warrior. The sun dance is a custom among the Indians which seeks to elevate a spirit of honour among men as well as women. No young woman dare take part in the sun dance unless she is virtuous, for she is sure to be pointed out and put to shame, and if she does not take part, then suspicion falls upon her and she is likewise put to shame. The men emulate the deeds of their fathers in order that they may take part in the sun dance. And thus this wonderful dance becomes a school for patriotism among the tribes and a stimulus to deeds of valour as well as an incentive to virtue. I do not think that anything has ever made a stronger impression upon me than the sun dance. It was always held in May, a beautiful time of the year, and as we young people watched the various phases of the dance, both young men and young women desired to do right that we might have our share in this wonderful ceremony."

This passing allusion to one of the great Indian rites and its influence upon Indian character may lead the reader to follow further into this weird enactment.

Another chieftain has been folded in his blanket. The war-bonnet and war-shirt he wears in the picture we made of him were laid beside him in his last sleep, emblems of his last battle and tokens of his final conquest.

Chief Bull Snake

Bull Snake

Old Bull Snake, or Snake Bull's, Indian name is Ear-Ous-Sah-Chee-dups, which means male snake. Years ago when far from camp he was bitten by a rattlesnake. The only companion with him did all within his power to save his friend. The death stupor was coming on, and his companion hurried to the camp with the tidings. His relations rushed to the rescue. He finally recovered and has ever since been called Bull Snake. It is a fitting appellation for this grizzled warrior of sixty-eight years. The bow and arrow became the plaything of his boyhood days. With it he sought the lair of wild things and shot with glee the buffalo calf; his final strength winging the arrow through the heart of the buffalo bull. Then came the days of the war trail, eager, savage days—days when the hated foe was pursued on foot and the warpath was followed for very love of war. This passion for war led him to the camp of General Crook, where he was assigned the task of trailing the hostile Sioux. The further story of Bull Snake is best told in his own words:

"At that time I must have been about twenty-three years old. We moved down to the Little Rosebud. I was the first of the scouts to discover the Sioux who were approaching us. After I reported, I mounted my horse and in company with two other scouts went over to locate the Sioux. We found ten Sioux and began to fight. My companions with both of their horses were killed. Then the battle of the Little Rosebud began. The Sioux and Cheyennes were all circling about us. General Crook sent for me. The entire command was surrounded. I thought it was my last day. I asked to be allowed to make a dash for a weak point in the line, his soldiers to follow. I did this and we broke through. Crook right flanked the enemy and won the day. In the counter attack two other Crows were on the ridge with me fighting. I raised my coup stick to strike a Sioux and he shot me, hitting my horse and we fell together. I found that I was badly wounded and could not stand up. I raised up as far as I could and fired three shots at the Sioux. There the battle ended."

War worn, halting on one foot, this savior of Crook's entire command presents a pitiful remnant of Indian valour. Speech more pathetic never came from the lips of any man: "The greatest thing to me is the education of my children. Since I was wounded, about thirty-six years ago, I have been thinking over my life. My leg has been weak and my heart has been sorry. I feel that I have suffered because I have followed my Great Father's order. I am glad I fought for the soldiers, for I think it was the right thing to do. Because of my wounded leg I am not able to work; sometimes I nearly starve, and yet I feel that I did the right thing. Will you be kind enough to see that I get my pension? I need it!" Be kind enough? Let the Government make answer in gratitude to the sagacious bravery of a red man bearing through life his daily burden of pain and the greater suffering of an unrequited heart who gloriously met the test of sacrifice.

Mountain Chief

Mountain Chief

Omaq-kat-tsa, carrying with it the meaning of Big Brave, is a name eminently fitting to Mountain Chief. The nobility of his presence, the Roman cast of his face, the keen penetration of his eye, the breadth of his shoulders, the dignity with which he wears the sixty-seven years of his life, all conspire to make this hereditary chief of the Fast Buffalo Horse band of the Blackfeet preeminent among the Indians and eminent among any class of men. He wears his hair on the left side in two braids; on the right side he wears one braid, and where the other braid should be, the hair hangs in long, loose black folds. He is very demonstrative. He acts out in pantomime all that he says.

He carries a tin whistle pendent to his necklace. First he is whistling, again he is singing, then he is on his hands and knees on the ground pawing up the dust like a buffalo when he is angry. His gestures are violent and his speech is guttural, like the sputtering of water from an exhaust. He sings a war song of his own composition and you can hear him for a mile. When asked to tell a story of his boyhood days he said that rather than tell such a story he would prefer to describe the management of the camp under the two great chiefs; his father, Mountain Chief, and Chief Lame Bull. These two men signed the treaty between the United States and the Blackfoot tribe, together with other tribes, in 1855, when Franklin Pierce was President. The historic information vouchsafed by Mountain Chief regarding the conduct of an Indian camp, their manner and method of hunting buffalo, and the purposes to which they put the buffalo, has never before been put in type:

"I remember the different chiefs in the camp when I was a boy, and how they governed the camp. My father, Mountain Chief, and his chum, Chief Lame Bull, were living in the same tepee. They each had a medicine pipe. These two chiefs made the plans before they moved the camp. After the plans were made, they took their medicine pipes and placed them against the rear side of the tepee. That indicated that the camp was going to remain for another day. The women of the camp were sent around by the various warriors to note the position of the pipes so they could tell what the plans were. When they came back, they told their husbands the pipes were in the rear of the tepee; then the husbands would say: 'The camp is going to remain for another day.' Then the chiefs sent for Four Bear, who asked certain Indians to go around and tell the people that the camp would remain for another day. Then Four Bear went toward the camp from the sunrise and walked around the camp toward the sunset. Then the Indians told their wives and children to keep still, and see what was going to be said. Four Bear would then tell the people that the camp would remain another day and to tell their wives to go after wood. Then the women took the travois and went after wood. Then the chiefs sent for the leaders and warriors; we called them 'crazy dogs.' The leaders of the crazy dogs came into the tepee of Mountain Chief and Lame Bull, and my father, Mountain Chief, told these two crazy dogs to start before sunrise, and to take with them the other crazy dogs to find where there was a lot of good fresh water, and a lot of grass where they might camp, and also where they might find the nearest herd of buffalo. The crazy dogs found a good place where there was plenty of buffalo and water, and then they marked the camp. When these crazy dogs found a location for the camp they were fortunate enough to find a big herd of buffalo. On their return, before they reached the camp they began to sing a crazy dog song, riding abreast. It means: 'A song to sharpen your knife, and patch up your stomach, for you are going to have something good to eat.' They made a circle, coming to camp from the sunrise, and moved toward the sunset, and then the leaders told the camp they had seen lots of buffalo. Then they dismounted and went home. After the crazy dogs had had their meal, they went over to the tepee of the chiefs; then they told the chiefs they had found a good camping place, good ground, good water, and a big herd of buffalo just beyond. The crazy dogs had their smoke, it was late when they went home, and then they sent for Four Bear. Four Bear went to the camp, told the people concerning their new camp, and the next morning the women took the medicine pipes and put them at the side of the tepee looking toward the direction where they were going to camp. Husbands told their wives to go out and see on which side of the tepee the medicine pipes were placed, that they might know where they were going. Then the wives came in and told them that the medicine pipes pointed in a northerly direction. The husbands told the wives that the camp was going to move north. The camp broke up that very morning. The chiefs and their wives sat by their tepees in a half circle, smoking while the camp was being broken up. After the chiefs were through smoking, they got up, and found the camp ready to move. They got a lot of mixed tobacco ready, and then they got on their horses. The chiefs started out in procession. After going some distance they halted; the crazy dogs followed, standing on each side, watching the movement of the camp to see that everybody was out. After everybody had left the camp, the chiefs followed the procession. When they thought it was noon they made a halt. They took their travois and saddles from the horses, and rested; then had their lunch. The chiefs then told Four Bear to get the camp in traveling shape again, and went on. Finally they came to the spot where the camping place was marked. They then took the medicine pipes and put them on a tripod, and the warriors came and sat around and smoked. Four Bear was then told to get the people settled, to tie up the buffalo horses, and get ready for the hunt. Four Bear then told the people not to get a meal but to get a little lunch, and get ready for the hunt. Then the chiefs started out for the buffalo, the hunters following. They stopped halfway before they got to the herd, and told all the hunters not to start for the buffalo until they were all ready and everybody had a fair chance. In the meantime one of the Indians sneaked away to crawl up toward the buffalo. Then this fellow chased the buffalo, and the crazy dogs took after him. When they got him, they broke his gun, his arrows and bow, broke his knife, cut his horse's tail off, tore off his clothes, broke his saddle in pieces, tore his robe in pieces, cut his rope into small bits, also his whip. Then they sent him off afoot. About that time the buffalo had stopped again, then the main body got on their horses, and started the chase. If a hunter hit a buffalo with one arrow, he gave a scream, and that indicated that he had hit him just once. There were very few guns in those days and those were flint-locks. Sometimes when a hunter rode side by side with a buffalo, and shot the animal, the arrow would go clear through. The Indians were very proud and careful of their arrows. They did not wish to break them. That is the reason why they shot them on the side, so that when the buffalo fell the arrow would not be broken. Lots of the buffalo fell on their knees, and would begin to move from side to side. Then the Indian, for fear that the arrow would be broken, jumped off his horse and pulled it out. The hunter then tied his horse to the horns of the buffalo for fear that he might be attacked by enemies at any moment. After this they took out their knives and sharpened them on hard steel, like the flint with which they made fire. All the time they were sharpening their knives they were looking around for the approach of the enemy. The fire steel was scarce, we had to use rocks most of the time. The knives we procured from the Hudson Bay Company. When we killed a buffalo bull, we placed him on his knees, then we began to skin him down the back of the neck, down the backbone, splitting it on each side. The cows we laid on their backs, and cut down the middle. We used the buffalo cowhide for buffalo robes; the buffalo bulls' hides were split down the back because from this hide we made war shields, parflesche bags, and saddle blankets. The husbands would tell the wives to take care of the heads. The wives took the brains out of the buffalo skull and mixed them with the largest part of the liver, and after mixing well, used the brains and liver in tanning the hides. Then the wife was told to take out the tripe and skin it, for they used the skin as a bucket with which to carry water when they got home. They had strips of rawhide about three feet long and a quarter of an inch wide and tied the meat so that they could carry it home on the horses. They took the backbone after it had been cleaned of the flesh, and tied the meat to that and threw it over the back of the horse so that the load would not hurt the back of the horse. When we got home with the meat we unloaded. The men who had gone without their wives simply got off their horses and went into the tepee. The women rushed out to get the meat. Then the women took the horse with the meat on it to their father-in-law. Then the mother-in-law hurried to get the meal, taking the ribs of the buffalo, setting them up against the fire to roast. After the meat was cooked it was cut in slices and placed in a wooden bowl, and the mother-in-law took the meat over to the lodge of her son-in-law. That was all we had for our meal. We had no coffee or anything else to eat, but we made a good meal from the meat of the buffalo. Then the son-in-law said to his wife: Your mother has been feeding me all the time, now you go out and catch that mare and give it to her as a present. There was plenty of meat in the camp and then we boys would go out and play buffalo. We would take a long piece of rawhide, fasten a piece of meat to it, and one of us would drag it along while the others fired arrows into it—the arrows we used for killing squirrels and birds. When we chased the boy dragging the piece of meat he would stop after we overtook him, and paw the dust and would imitate the buffalo bull, and pick up the piece of meat and swing it round his head, all the while we were trying to shoot arrows into it. But sometimes in the swinging of the meat with the arrows in it a boy would get hit, and then he would run back and fall down, and we would run back to him and say that he had been hooked. He would be groaning all the time. Then we would pick up weeds and squeeze the juice out of them, acting as though we were doctors. About that time night came on, and the chiefs sent for Four Bear, and Four Bear would go around and tell the people that the grass in that camp was pretty well taken up. The next morning the women would take their medicine pipes and put them on the side, indicating where the next camp was going to be, and thus we went on from camp to camp."

"The years have passed on, and now the old warriors and myself get together and talk about the old buffalo days, and we feel very lonesome. We talk over the camping places, and the old days of the chase, and the events of those times, and we feel glad again. When we think of the old times we think also of the white man for it was their arms that made the buffalo extinct. If the Indians had had nothing but arrows, the buffalo would be left to-day. We blame the Government again, for they told the agents not to sell ammunition to the Indians, and they sold this ammunition on the sly. This was done so that the Indians could get the hides for the traders."

"The greatest event in my life was in the war of the Black-feet against the Crees, at Hope Up, Canada. My horse and myself were both covered with blood. Let me tell you about this battle. The war was between the Blackfeet and the Crees. The camp was on Old Man's River. The bands were so many that they were camped on every bend of the river. My father, Mountain Chief, was at the upper end of the camp. I was twenty-two years old at the time. It was in the fall of the year, and the leaves had all fallen. The lower camp was attacked by the Crees at night. The people were just getting up in the morning when the news came that the lower camp had been attacked by the Crees. I got my best horse; it was a gray horse. My father led his band in company with Big Lake who that summer had been elected a big chief. We rode up over the ridge while in the plain below the battle was raging. As we rode down the hill slope, I began to sing my war song. I carried the shield in my hand and this song that I sung belonged to that shield. One of the medicine men dreamed that whoever held this shield would not be hit by the bullets. While singing I put in the words: 'My body will be lying on the plains.' When I reached the line of battle I did not stop, but rode right in among the Crees, and they were shooting at me from behind and in front. When I rode back the same way the men made a break for the coulee. As soon as the men got into the coulee they dug a pit. I was lying about ten yards away on the side of the hill. I was singing while lying there. I could not hear on account of the roar of the guns, and could not see for the smoke. About that time they heard my whistle, and the Crees made a break for the river. Then the Blackfeet made an onrush for the Crees and I ran over two of them before they got to the river. As they were crossing the river I jumped off my horse and took my spear and stabbed one of the Crees between the shoulders. He had a spear and I took that away from him. I jumped off my horse again, and just as I returned there was a Cree who raised his gun to fire at me. I ran over him, and he jumped up and grabbed my horse by the bridle. I swung my horse's head around to protect myself and took the butt of my whip and knocked him down. When I struck him he looked at me and I found that his nose had been cut off. I heard afterward that a bear had bitten his nose off. After I knocked him down, I killed him. I jumped on my horse and just then I met another Cree. We had a fight on our horses; he shot at me and I shot at him. When we got close together I took his arrows away from him, and he grabbed me by the hair of the head. I saw him reach for his dagger, and just then we clinched. My war-bonnet had worked down on my neck, and when he struck at me with his dagger it struck the war-bonnet, and I looked down and saw the handle sticking out, and grabbed it and killed the other Indian. Then we rushed the Crees into the pit again, and my father came up with one of the old muskets and handed it to me. It had seven balls in it, and when I fired it it kicked so hard it almost killed me. I feel that I had a more narrow escape by shooting that gun than I had with the Indians. When we returned I had taken nine different scalps. The Crees who had not been scalped had taken refuge in the scant forest, and my father said to quit and go home. So we took pity on the tribe, and let them go, so they could tell the story. I remember that we killed over three hundred, and many more that I cannot remember. When we returned we began to count how many we had killed. We crossed the creek and went to the pit, and they were all in a pile. Then we were all singing around the pit, and I put in the words, 'The guns, they hear me.' And everybody turned and looked at me, and I was a great man after that battle. Then we went home and began to talk about the battle, and the Indians who were dead. There never was any peace between the Crees and the Black-feet; they were always bitter enemies. When the battle began, the leader of the Crees came right up to our tepee and slit it, and said: 'You people are sleeping yet, and I came,' I fired a gun and killed him. The Crees took their knives and slit the tepees of our village down the sides and then rushed in. When the Crees rushed into the tepees they took everything they could lay their hands on, killing the women and children, and that made me mad. That was why I fought so hard that day."

War Memories

Mountain Chief's Boyhood Sports

"I remember when I was a boy how we used to trap foxes. We all got together and took our sisters along, took the axe, went into the woods and cut willows, tied them up in bundles, and put them on our backs, our sisters doing the same thing. We would go to the east of the camp, where the smoke and all of the scent would go, find a snowdrift in the coulee and unload our packs. The first thing we did was to stamp on the snow—to see if it was solid. We would drive four sticks into the snow, and while driving in the sticks we would sing: 'I want to catch the leader.' The song is a fox song to bring good luck. As far as I can remember I got this story from my grandfather. There was an old man in the camp who went to the mountains, and stayed there for four days without anything to eat in order that he might get his dream. A fox came to him and told him: 'This is one way you can kill us,' and this is why we put in this song while we were making the deadfall. After we got through fixing up our deadfall we returned home, a boy in the lead, then a girl, then a boy, then a girl, and while we were returning to the camp we sang the fox song, putting in these words: 'I want to kill the leader.' Then we fell down, imitating the fox in the trap. When we got back to camp we took buffalo meat, covering it with fat and roasted it a while so that the fox would get the scent. Then we took the bait and put it on a stick and put it over our left arm, and then the boys and girls all went back again, singing as we went; 'We hope to have good luck.' This song was a good-luck song. After we put the bait in the trap we all went home silently, not saying a word. But before we went to bed my mother said to me: 'I am going to get a piece of dried beef without any fat, and you take it over to the old man who always has good luck in trapping foxes, and he will pray for you that you may have good luck.' When the dried meat was done, I took it over to the old man, gave it to him, and asked him to pray for me that I might have good luck. The old fellow would then start to say his prayers for me. The old man to whom he prayed was the old man that dreamed how to kill the fox. The old man told me to pick up four stones about five inches long, and tie them with a string. He tied a stone on each wrist, one behind my neck, and one at the back of my belt. Then he took charcoal and blackened my nose on each side to represent the fox, then he made me take off my clothes; he took a stick about five feet long and held it in an inclined position. The old man then took two sticks and hit them together, and stood right by the door singing. He told me to whistle; then he walked toward the point where he had held the sticks. He then lay down by the stick and began to scratch on the ground as though he were caught in a trap. Then he said: 'You are going to catch one now.' By this time it was pretty late in the night. We gave a signal to the other boys and girls to come out and we all went to see our traps. I had a robe made out of a yearling calfskin that I threw over me, and I also had a rope my mother gave me with which to drag the foxes home if I caught any. Then we went to our traps, following the same path as we did when we went to set the trap with bait. As we went along we filled the night with song, singing: 'The fox is in a trap, and his tail is sticking out.' When we got near the traps we stopped singing, and one of us went on ahead. The leader who went ahead walked straight to our trap, when he returned he whistled; then we knew that some of us had caught something. When he came back he pointed out certain ones who had caught foxes. Then we lifted our deadfalls, slipped the ropes over them, and dragged them home. As we approached the camp we formed in line abreast, and began to sing. When we reached the camp every one was in bed. We sang the song which indicated that we had caught something; then we imitated the cry of the crow and the magpie, which indicated that we had had extra good luck. If we imitated the hooting of an owl, it showed that we had had bad luck, and none of us had caught anything. We were always anxious to catch some wild game, because we sold the skins to the traders, and with the money we bought knives and brass earrings and beads and paint."

Chief Red Cloud

Chief Red Cloud

Chief Red Cloud, head chief of the Ogallallas, was without doubt the most noted and famous chief at the time of his death, December, 1909, in the United States. He became famous through his untiring efforts in opposition to everything the Government attempted to do in the matter of the pacification of the Sioux. One of the most lurid pages in the history of Indian warfare records the massacre at Fort Phil Kearny, in December, 1866. Chief Red Cloud planned and executed this terrific onslaught. He always remained a chief. He was always the head of the restless element, always the fearless and undaunted leader. He was the Marshal Ney of the Indian nations, until sickness and old age sapped his vitality and ambition.

The holding of the last Great Indian Council occurred a little less than two months before his death. Blind and bedridden he could not attend the council. During the last few shattered years of his warrior life, he relegated all the powers of chieftainship to his son, now fifty-four years of age. The younger Chief Red Cloud attended the council. He is tall and straight and lithe, and possesses a splendid military bearing. He is a winsome speaker, and his words are weighted with the gold of Nature's eloquence. Every attitude of his body carries the charm of consummate grace, and when he talks to you there is a byplay of changing lights in his face that becomes fascinating. Like his father he was a born leader and warrior. His story of the Custer fight and his participation in it may be found in the chapter on that subject. Regarding his own life he tells us:

"It has been a part of my life to go out on the warpath, ever since I was fourteen years old. As you know it is a part of our history that the man who goes on the warpath and kills the most enemies gets a coup stick, and the coup stick is the stepping-stone to become a chief. I remember my first war party was forty-one years ago. This battle was at Pryor Creek against the Crows. I was in four great battles, with my father, Chief Red Cloud. At the battle of Pryor Creek I captured many horses, and took three scalps. Thirty-four years ago I killed four Crows and earned my coup stick. I kept these scalps until my visit to Washington when some white man wanted them."

"I want to speak about the buffalo. There were plenty of buffalo and deer when I was a young man, but the white man came and frightened all the game away, and I blame the white man for it. By order of our Great Father in Washington the buffalo were all killed. By this means they sought to get the Sioux Indians back to their reservation."

"The greatest event in my life I may explain in this way: Years ago I had been trained to go on the warpath. I loved to fight; I was fighting the Indians and fighting the soldiers. Then there came a time when the Great Father said we must stop fighting and go to school, we must live in peace, that we were Indian brothers, and must live in peace with the white man. I believe that the greatest event in my life was when I stopped the old Indian custom of fighting and adopted what the white man told me to do—live in peace."

The hoar frosts of autumn had touched into opal and orange the leaves of the forest until great banners of colour lined the banks of the swiftly flowing

Little Big Horn; the camp of the last Great Indian Council lifted cones of white on the edge of these radiant trees. Sombre winds uttered a melancholy note through the dying reeds on the river bank, and all of it seemed a prelude to an opening grave, and significant of the closing words uttered to me by Chief Red Cloud:

"My father, old Chief Red Cloud, has been a great fighter against the Indians, and against the white man, but he learned years ago to give up his fighting. He is now an old man, ready to die, and I am sorry that he could not come here. It is now over five years since he gave me his power and I became chief, and he and I both are glad that we are friends to the white man and want to live in peace."

Chief Two Moons

Chief Two Moons

Chief Two Moons wears about his neck an immense cluster of bear claws. His arms are also encircled with this same insignia of distinction. Although he has reached the age of nearly threescore years and ten, his frame is massive and his posture, when standing, typifies the forest oak. It takes no conjuring of the imagination to picture this stalwart leader of the Cheyennes against Custer on that fateful June day, as suffering no loss in comparison with the great generals who led the Roman eagles to victory. Two Moons is now nearly blind; he carries his coup stick, covered with a wolfskin, both as a guide for his footsteps and a badge of honour. There is not a tinge of gray in the ample folds of his hair, and his voice is resonant and strong. His story of the Custer fight, told for me at the cross marking the spot where Custer fell, to be found in the Indians' story of that battle, is both thrilling and informing.

Here Custer Fell

Seated around the campfire in my tepee while a cold rain sifted through the canvas, Two Moons became reminiscent. His mother and brother were called Two Moons, meaning two months—in the Indian tongue, Ish-hay-nishus. His mind seemed to travel back to his boyhood days, for he started right in by saying: "When a Cheyenne boy wants to marry a young woman it takes a long time for them to get acquainted with each other. When he wants to marry a girl or have her for a sweetheart he tells another fellow with whom he is acquainted, and who is also acquainted with the girl, and this young man goes and tells her, the same as a white man writes to the young lady on paper. And this Indian friend brings them together; this Indian goes and tells the girl that the boy wants to be a sweetheart to her, and the girl will say,

'Well, I will think it over.' And then she thinks it over, and finally says if he comes to see her some time in the day or night then she will believe that he is a sweetheart of hers. So then the young man goes to the young girl, and talks to her, and they make up their minds to get married. They get married after this fashion: the young man may go to the tent of the girl at night and the girl may come out, then the boy will take the girl away to his home. So then the next morning the young man's folks and family bring their presents. They take two or three horses, good horses, and load these horses up with good stuff, clothes, shawls, necklaces, bracelets, and moccasins. Then they take the girl back to her home. The girl's family divides up the presents after they get home."

"There is another way: When an old man and woman decide they want a grandchild, they tell their son they are going to buy a certain girl and he must marry her. Then another Indian goes and tells the girl's family that they would like to trade for the girl, and if it is all right he goes back and the boy's people load up some horses with goods, and take them over to the girl's folks. And then they take her back and give her to the boy's family. The bride was bedecked with brass rings which were taken from the tepee, but they used other rings for engagement rings after the white man came."

In speaking of death, Two Moons said: "If the person who dies has a mother or father or friend, they all cry, and all the things that belonged to the boy they give away to other people. They dig a grave in between the rocks and put the body in the ground and cover it up with dirt and rocks. They always dig a grave for a person who dies whether they have friends or folks. The old people believed there was a man came on earth here and some of his children had done a lot of crime and fooling with him, and they talked of his going up to heaven, and living there and looking down, and that is where we will all go when we die. Also the old people believed that that man said: 'There will be a kind of cross light up in the sky, which will mark the path for souls on the road.' 'High White Man' is our name for God. And it was the son of High White Man who told this, and who created us and made everything."

"The first time the Indian saw a locomotive, he called it the Iron Horse, and the railroad was called the Iron Road. The old people first saw what they called white men, and they called the white man a Ground Man. I was so young then that I did not know anything at that time. I saw some men driving an ox team, or carrying packs on their backs and walking. When I got older most of the people knew that these white men were good. The first time they saw a white man they called him Drive-a-Wagon. They did not know what they were hauling, but found out afterward that it was sugar and coffee. I remember how pleased I was when I first saw sugar and coffee. When I was a boy the Indians used to get the grains of coffee and put it in a bucket and boil it, and it would never cook at all. Finally a white man came along and took the coffee and put it in a bucket and put it on the coals without any water, and stirred it until it turned brown, and then he took it off and mashed it up between two stones, and that was how we learned to make coffee. I like it, and have always liked it."

"The white man is to blame for the driving away of the buffalo." (It will here be observed that the Indian cannot talk very long at a time without this ever recurring subject being forced to the front.) "After the white man had driven the buffalo away, a great council among the Indians was held; all the tribes possible were called to this big council on the Platte River. All the different tribes were there. A white man came there and brought a lot of stuff, such as clothes, plates, guns, coffee grinders, knives, blankets, and food, and gave them to the Indians. They also brought shoes. This man said that he wanted some Indians to go to Washington. They went down the Missouri River. They went by ox team from the Platte River to the Missouri, and then by ship down the Missouri River. These men were gone to Washington for a year; they came back about the middle of the summer. The President told the Indians they were his grandchildren, and thus the Indians called the President their grandfather. Grandfather told them that a white man would come and live with them, and that for fifty-five years they would get clothes and food. I was nine years old when they held the council and ten years old when they came back. From the time of the council the old people settled down in the Black Hills and in the south and quit running around. From that time all the Indians became friends of the white man, and the white man bought the buffalo hides and other skins. After they settled down everything went along all right until I was fifteen years old, and then the whites came in and there was a fight between the whites and Cheyennes and some other tribes of Indians. I do not know what happened, but some Cheyennes went over to the white man's camp on Shell River, and the white men started to fire at the Indians. That was the cause of the trouble that year. Later the Comanches and Apaches and Kiowas fought among themselves, and came north to fight the Cheyennes. We called them the Texas Indians. Then the wars between the tribes and the hostilities between the Red and White grew less and less. There was a man named Honey;—the Indians called him Bee— he told the Cheyennes they must not fight. In the numerous battles in which I was engaged I received many wounds. I was wounded by the Pawnee Indians in a fight with them, by an arrow; wounded again at Elk River in the Yellowstone, when I was shot through the arm by a Crow of the Big Horn. I was wounded again on the Crow River in Utah in a fight with the United States soldiers, when I was shot through the thigh. I had my horse shot through the jaw in a fight with the Crows, but to-day I am a friend of all the tribes; once I was their enemy. I was told by General Miles at Fort Kearny that we must not fight any more, that it was the orders from Washington. I remember General Miles well. I know him and I am a friend of his. When

General Miles told me what I ought to do, it was just as though he put me in his hand and showed me the white man and the Indian, and told us we were all to be good friends, so that is the reason General Miles' name is a great name among the Cheyennes as well as the whites. And your coming among us is just like General Miles; you are helping the Indians and can help them. They need help for they are all poor. After the Indians settled down and General Miles had told us what the Great Father at Washington wanted, and after I had succeeded in settling the Indians, the order came from Washington that we should take up land and call it a claim. So I looked all around for land on which to settle; then I went over to Tongue River on the Rosebud so that my family and children could be reared and have a home. All that I have told you is true. General Miles told me that when I settled down and took this land, there might be some people who would come along and try to cheat us out of our land, but not to pay any attention to them, that it was our land. There are a great many people settled in Montana in the land that belonged to the Indians. These people are raising lots of cattle and ought to be good to the Indian. I have been on this land for over twenty years, but we are not yet accustomed to the white man's food: we love the meat yet, and we long for the buffalo. There is a great deal of land leased by cattle men in Montana, and the money ought to go to buy more cattle for the Indian, and clothes for our children. I like to tell the truth just as I have seen it with my own eyes, and I will have another good story for you to-morrow night. I am getting old, but when I begin to talk about the old times I think I am young again, and that I am the biggest of them all."

Custer Scouts

THE STORY OF THE SURVIVING CUSTER SCOUTS

Too little stress has been laid upon the values accruing to the safety and success of the United States troops, in their warfare on the western frontier, from the services of Indian scouts.

A wild and often inaccessible country to traverse, with none of the aids of electricity or modern travel; with difficult mountain ranges to climb, blinding blizzards and insufferable cold, blistering heat, and the hazards of unknown rivers to cross through banks of perilous quicksands; stupendous distances to travel, and all the time an alert, wily, and masterful foe lurking in any one of ten thousand impregnable coverts—this is a hint of the scout's life. These brave and tireless scouts led not to ambush but to the advantage of our men at arms. Estimate the bravery, the sagacity, the perseverance, the power of endurance displayed by these Indian scouts, and their superlative service will call for our patriotic gratitude. No trial of strength and endurance, no test of bravery, no audacity of peril, hindered or made them afraid. They were more important than guns and munitions of war. The Crows made the best scouts, for two reasons: They had never taken up arms against the whites; all the neighbouring tribes battled against the Crows for the conquest of their land. The Crow scouts, therefore, aided the United States soldiers to conquer and drive out their hereditary foes that they might preserve their land and their homes. It was therefore not only a fight of fidelity and fealty but of preservation—Nature's strongest law.

Our story is now concerned with the four surviving scouts who led the United States soldiers in many campaigns under Crook, Terry, Miles, Howard, and finally Custer. The Indians who piloted Long Hair to the great Sioux camp in the valley of the Little Big Horn—the last day of life for Custer, the last contest at arms for the Indians—are now old men, and their own life record is full of thrilling interest.

White Man Runs Him—Custer Scout

White-Man-Runs-Him

This red man of the plains is a veritable Apollo Belvedere. He is pronounced by all ethnologists as possessing a physique hardly paralleled by any of the northern tribes. He fulfills in his life the nobility of his stature. At the age of sixty-five, his figure, seventy-four inches in height, stands unbent—supple and graceful. His whole aspect is that of quiet dignity, his voice is soft and musical, his eye is keen and penetrating; modestly and earnestly he describes his share in the Custer fight. He was trustworthy to the point of death. Very many times the safety of an entire command depended upon his caution and sagacity. He served as scout under Terry, Crook, and Custer.

While telling his story he stood upright, lifted his hands full length, which among the Crows signified an oath, meaning that he would tell the truth. His Indian boyhood name was Be-Shay-es-chay-e-coo-sis, "White Buffalo That Turns Around." When he was about ten years of age his grandfather named him after an event in his own father's life. A white man pursued his father, firing his gun above his father's head in order to make him run. And he was afterward called "White-Man-Runs-Him."

Regarding his boyhood days he tells us: "Until I was fifteen years of age, together with my boy playmates, we trained with bows and arrows. We learned to shoot buffalo calves, and this practice gave us training for the warpath. It answered two purposes: protection and support. We were also taught the management of horses. We early learned how to ride well. When the camp moved we boys waited and walked to the new camp for exercise, or we hunted on the way. We felt brave enough to meet anything. Thus it was that we roamed over the hills, and climbed the rocks in search of game, but we were sure to arrive at the camp just in time for the meal which had been prepared by the squaws. If on our way to the camp we came across game, such as a rabbit, we shot it with our arrows, broiled it and ate it for fun. When we got to the new camp we would all praise one boy for some deed that he had performed on the way, and then we would sing and dance. That boy's folks would give all us boys a dish of pemmican for the good deed he had performed. The little girls had small tepees. They practised cooking, learning from the older women. These girls would serve delicacies to us, and we would sing and dance around their tepee."

"When we were quite small boys we would go out hunting horses, and bring back a dog and call it a horse. When we made a new camp we seldom stayed more than ten days. In that way our health was sustained by travel. While we were on the move from one camp to another, we had to cross wide streams. We boys would measure the width of the river, and compete with each other to see who could swim across without stopping. I am telling you now what I did to build myself up to be the man I am now. The boys who were the same age and size as myself would wrestle, and if a boy downed me three or four times, I kept up the practice of wrestling until I had more strength. Then I could throw this boy and I was satisfied. I selected a boy to run a race; if the boy passed me, then I made the distance longer, and if he passed me again, I made the distance still longer, for I knew that I was long-winded. Then I won the race."

"Fifteen or twenty of us boys would go out to the river, and daub ourselves up with mud and so disguise ourselves that no one in the camp would know us. Then we would take jerked buffalo beef that the women had hung up around the camp to dry and go off out of sight and have a feast. None of us was caught at it, because they could not tell one boy from another. During this time I watched what old people did. When I came to grow up, I went forth equipped. I always had an amibition to do more than the best man in the camp could do. When I went on the chase, I made up my mind that I would bring home a buffalo or I would not go home. And my folks rejoiced, believing that they had a good boy to help support the family."

"We were surrounded by many different tribes, Shoshones, Sioux, Piegans, and Gros Ventres. They were all our enemies. We often went on the warpath against these people, because they were always trying to take our horses and conquer our land. When we went on the warpath sometimes we would stop and kill a buffalo and have a feast. If we could, we crawled up on the enemy's camp and stole his horses. If we met a foe we tried to kill him and bring his scalp home."

"Our custom of painting was a sign. If in a dream we saw any one painted, that was our medicine. In our dreams we would see various kinds of paints and how to use them; we would see certain birds and feathers, and we adopted this as our style of paint. Others would try to buy from us our style of paint. The kind of paint and feathers we wore made us brave to do great deeds—to kill the enemy or take his horses. We did not buy horses, but stole them. We gave the horses to our relations. If I got one or more horses, it represented so much value to me, and brought honour to me. And, besides, the girls admired the man who could go out and get horses, and in this way we won a wife. After marriage I would sell a horse, buy elk teeth, beaded leggings, and put them on my wife as a wedding present. Elk teeth and horses were a sign of wealth. Then my wife would make a tepee, and put it up; then I would settle down and have a home."

"In early days we had nothing for clothing except the skins of animals. We used the buffalo hide or the deer hide for a breechclout. For a bucket we used the tripe of the buffalo, after thoroughly cleaning it. We would hang it up on the branch of a tree, full of water, and drink out of it."

"The white people came long before I was born, but when I first remember the white man I thought he was very funny. I never knew of any one person particularly, but I know there are good white people and bad white people, honest white people and dishonest white people, true white people and mean white people. We always take it for granted that what the white people say is true, but we have found out by experience that they have been dishonest with us and that they have mistreated us. Now when they say anything we think about it, and sometimes they are true. I am saying this about the white people in general."

"Going back to the days when we had no horses, we would see the buffalo on the plains; we then surrounded them, driving them as we did so, near to the edge of some steep precipice. When we got the buffalo up near the edge of the precipice we would all wave our blankets and buffalo robes and frighten the buffalo and they would run off the steep place, falling into the valley below, one on top of another. Of course the undermost animals were killed. Then we would go down and get them and take away the meat."

"The Indians found some dogs on the prairie. After they got the dogs they would fasten a pole on either side of the dogs with a tanned hide fastened between the poles, and the Indians would put their trappings, their meat, and their pappooses on this hide stretched between the poles. In that way they moved from place to place, the dog carrying the utensils of the camp. We called it a travois. One day when we were moving, the dog who was carrying a baby in the travois saw a deer and ran after it. He went over a bank and carried the baby with him, and finally came back without the baby."

"In counting the dead on the battlefield we placed sticks by the dead soldiers or Indians, then gathered the sticks up, took them to one place in a pile and there counted the sticks. We count by fixing events in our mind. We have a brain and a heart, and we commit to memory an event, and then we say Chief So-and-So died when we broke camp on the Big Horn, and So-and-So were married when we had the big buffalo hunt in the snow. Or we had a big fight with the Sioux when our tepees were placed in a ring in the bend of the Yellowstone River. We dated our time from these events."

Folklore Tale—Crow

"When I was a little boy this is a story that was told around every campfire: It was called 'Old Man Coyote!' Before the white man came the coyote used to roam over all the land. The Old Man Coyote took the little coyotes he picked up on the prairies and called them his little brothers. The little coyote was such a sly animal that the old coyote always sent him on errands, because he knew he would always be up to something. The Old Man Coyote says: 'We are alone: let us make man.' He said: 'Go and bring me some mud so that I can make a man, so that we can be together.' The Old Man Coyote took the mud and put it together, and put hair on it, and set it up on the ground, and said: 'There is a man!' The little coyote said: 'Make some more.' And the Old Man Coyote made four—two were women and two were men. The Old Man sized them up and said they were good, and so he made a whole lot more. Old Man Coyote said: 'It is good that we live together, and I want you to open each other's eyelids.' Old Man Coyote said to these people whom he had made: 'Now, if you stay together and are good to each other, you will be happy, and you will increase in numbers.' Old Man Coyote was our creator. Old Man Coyote said to these people whom he had made: 'This is your land; live here, eat of the fruit of the trees, drink of the rivers, hunt the game, and have a good time.' From that we believe that the white people had nothing to do with the land—it belonged to the Indian. This story, told to our people so many times, and told to me since I can remember, led me to believe when I came to know and understand that this land was wholly ours, and belonged entirely to the Indians. Old Man Coyote, after he had created man and woman, did not have anything to do, so he made a bow and arrow. He took the flint for the arrowhead, and with it he killed the buffalo. Then he gave the bow and arrow to the Indian and said to him: 'This is your weapon.' The people whom Old Man Coyote created had no knife, so he took the shoulder blade of the buffalo and sharpened it and made it into a knife. These people whom Old Man Coyote had created roamed round over the land and they found a mule. It was a great big mule with great big ears, and when they brought it home the people were all afraid of it. They all gathered around the mule, staring in amazement at him, and said: 'What kind of an animal is this? It is a dangerous animal.' Just then the mule stuck up his ears, and let out an awful cry, just such a cry as only the mule can make. Then the people all ran away as hard as they could go, scared almost to death, except one Indian, who fell flat on the earth—too scared to run. And finally the people called this man, 'Not-Afraid-of-the-Mule.' And in this way we learned how to name our Indians."

Hairy Moccasin—Custer Scout

Hairy Moccasin

Isapi-Wishish is the name the Indians called Hairy Moccasin, a scout under Gibbon, Miles, Howard, and Custer. His frame is small and wiry, and like his brother scout, Goes-Ahead, he too will soon be numbered with the great army of the dead. Silent, unobtrusive, carrying no mark of distinction, his moccasined feet move slowly along the path made by others. It must be noted that however unprepossessing his personality he wears an untarnished badge for bravery and faithful service as a scout. White-Man-Runs-Him said: "I cannot say anything better about Hairy Moccasin than to say that he executed faithfully the orders of General Custer." He was the boyhood playmate of White-Man-Runs-Him. They were companions in all the sports and games and tricks of the camp. When the Custer scouts traversed the difficult and dangerous route from the Little Rosebud to the valley where they located the mighty camp of the Sioux, it was Hairy Moccasin who under the stars of that June night reached the apex of the hills at dawn. The other scouts lay down to rest. Hairy Moccasin, leaving the others asleep, went to the summit—which is called the Crow's Nest—and as the gray streaks of the dawn began to silver the east, it was Moccasin's eye which caught the vision of the myriads of white tents, of the brown hills in the distance covered with brown horses, the curling smoke from hundreds of wigwams. Word was sent back to Custer. In excited tones, he asked: "Have you seen the cut-throat Sioux?" From the vantage point of the hills where they had seen the camp Hairy Moccasin was sent still farther in advance to reconnoitre. He climbed a pine-clad hill, found the Sioux everywhere, and then he rode back and reported to General Custer the size and position of the camp. On hearing the report Custer hurried up his command. As the brave general moved out of the valley up the ridge it is the testimony of White-Man-Runs-Him that Hairy Moccasin rode immediately in advance of Custer, and when the Cheyennes came up, "He fired at them, banged and banged at them, and the Cheyennes were afraid of Moccasin. They were afraid of all three of us. Custer would have been killed before the time he was shot if it had not been for Hairy Moccasin and myself, who were around him shooting at the Indians." When the United States soldiers were fighting the Nez Perces Hairy Moccasin got a horse away from the enemy, and brought it into the camp of the soldiers. Hairy Moccasin was always on the warpath performing brave deeds. The name and fame of Custer will live in the archives of his country, and a fadeless lustre will forever crown the heroic deeds of this Indian Scout.

Curly—Custer Scout

Curly

Curly, a Reno Crow, was born on the Little Rosebud, Montana, and is fifty-seven years of age. He has the bearing, grace and dignity of an orator. His name will also go down in history as one of the leading scouts who trailed for General Custer the Indian camp, and as the last of his scouts on the fated field where Custer and his command were slain. At times he is taciturn and solemn, and then bubbles over with mirthfulness. At the council held on the Crow Reservation, in October, 1907, with reference to the opening of unoccupied lands, Curly uttered this eloquent speech:

"I was a friend of General Custer. I was one of his scouts, and will say a few words. The Great Father in Washington sent you here about this land. The soil you see is not ordinary soil—it is the dust of the blood, the flesh, and bones of our ancestors. We fought and bled and died to keep other Indians from taking it, and we fought and bled and died helping the whites. You will have to dig down through the surface before you can find nature's earth, as the upper portion is Crow. The land, as it is, is my blood and my dead; it is consecrated, and I do not want to give up any portion of it."

Accompanied by a group of Indians, Curly came to my tepee when we were camped on the Little Big Horn. The whole company were greatly agitated because an Indian possessed with the spirit of self-importance had gone to Washington to make war against other Indians in the tribe who were industrious and loyal home builders. They all made speeches around the campfire, asking my interposition at Washington. In his argument Curly said: "Which man would you believe, the man who is trying to raise wheat for the people to get flour and bread from, oats to feed his horses, who builds a house for the shelter and preservation of his family, builds a stable in which to shelter his horses, tills the soil to get the product, trying to raise vegetables so that his people may have something to eat in summer and winter, or the man who would come along and run over this man who was working and trying to do something for his family, and would not work himself, but just run around and make a renegade of himself, quarrelling with his mother and brothers—which man would you believe? A man who quarrels with his mother is not fit for any duty." Gems like these would grace any brightest page of literature, but they are the everyday eloquence of the Indian.

Curly said regarding his early life: "When I was a boy I did not do much. I was not crazy, but I did not run into mischief. My father and mother always advised me not to get into mischief. My first remembrance of the white man was when I took the skins of buffalo calves into the trading stores and traded with the white man. I thought that was a great thing to do. I had been many times on the trail of the buffalo and had sought opportunity to go on the warpath. When I was about eighteen years old the Crow chiefs made the announcement that there were some United States officers in camp who wanted some Crow scouts. I quickly volunteered. My brother approached us after we started and took myself and Hairy Moccasin and White Swan and told us that we had a secret mission in another district. My brother was then on the warpath. We went as far with my brother as Tongue River and did not see what we were searching for and we came back home. Then the Crow scouts left the agency and camped at Clark's Ford, and Bonnie Bravo and Little Face, Indian scouts and interpreters, met us there. These scouts took us over to General Terry's camp again. The scouts who were with Terry had no horses, for the Sioux had captured them. We had with us eight horses.

Then we marched down as far as the Little Rosebud. There one of Terry's officers told us we were to go out and scout for the Sioux camp. We went as far as Tongue River, and Bonnie Bravo was the first one to discover the Sioux camp. Then we came back to the command and reported. General Terry moved his cavalry forward and attempted to ford the Yellowstone River. The water was so high that many of the men and horses were drowned, and the rest came back. Then Terry asked the scouts to go forward again, and see if the camp was still there. We found that the camp had moved from Tongue River up on the Little Rosebud. After that we reported, and General Terry did not say very much. General Terry then sent Bonnie Bravo and the two scouts back to the camp to procure horses. They sent two other scouts and the army wagons to Crow Agency for provisions. The soldiers did not leave the camp very far for fear of attack by the Sioux, for they kept close watch on them constantly, firing at any soldiers they saw. Then General Terry sent me toward Crow Agency to meet the wagons and the men who were with the horses. After we had met the wagons we stayed there all night and then went on to camp. General Terry then moved his camp, following the Yellowstone down. We were taken clear down to the mouth of the Powder River. White-Man-Runs-Him and another scout did not have any horses, so they got into the boat and went down the river, bringing a dispatch to Terry. The dispatch told us to go back and follow the Yellowstone up again. We went back and camped within ten or twelve miles of the mouth of the Big Horn, near where we had camped before. We stayed there three or four days, and then a steamboat arrived bringing Bouyer, the scout. He told us all to break camp. There were six of us who did the most of the scouting, and out of the six Terry told three of us to go and find the enemy's camp. General Terry and the commander of the infantry were in the ambulance, and Bouyer was there talking with them. Terry sent for Yellow Shield, then Yellow Shield sent for me. Bouyer then asked me who among the Crow scouts did the most scouting. I said White Swan, Hairy Moccasin, and myself. These scouts then camp up and joined me. Yellow Shield then told us that he wanted six men in all. Then we had a conference. We thought of White-Man-Runs-Him, but he had no horse. Then Yellow Shield said he would call White-Man-Runs-Him and Goes-Ahead to join us. After they had called these men they put us on the steamboat and sent us down the river, sending the other Crows home. We were taken down to the mouth of the Little Rosebud by the Yellowstone. We were told after we had had our dinner that we must dress ourselves up and paint up and get ready to scout."

Curly at this point reaches the camp of General Custer, and the remainder of the fascinating story of this warrior, orator, and scout, who followed with unfailing fidelity the fortunes of the United States soldiers, will be told in the chapter on "The Indians' Story of the Custer Fight."

Goes Ahead—Custer Scout

Goes-Ahead-Basuk-Ore

Goes-Ahead carries about a tall, attenuated, and weakened frame. He is standing on the verge of yonder land. He is stricken with a fatal disease. In manner he is as quiet and unobtrusive as a brooding bird. When reminiscent his wonted smile disappears, his eye lights up with a strange mysterious fire. He talks straight on like a man who has something to tell and is eager to tell it. We may gain better glimpses of his life if we let him tell his own tale:

"When I was quite a lad I went to war. I was the first in the battle and the others all said: 'There he goes ahead of us.' I have been first in battle ever since and thus I got my name, Goes-Ahead. The greatest pleasure I had when I was a boy, I remember, was in killing wolves. After we had shot the wolf we would run up and put our coup stick on him and play that he was our enemy. Another sport we had was playing buffalo. We divided up and part of the boys would be buffalo and part would be hunters. The boys who were playing buffalo would paw up the dust and we would run after them and shoot arrows at them, and then the buffalo bull would chase us back until he caught one of the boys, then we went on until we conquered the buffalo. When I was a young man we had buffalo skulls with the meat and skin all taken off and we would tie ropes to them and put them on the ice. The girls would sit on the buffalo head and we would draw them along the ice. That was one of our greatest pleasures. I was about fifteen years old when I first went on the war trail. It was in the winter time and I was on foot. I used a bow and arrows and my arrows were not very good. The young fellows who went with me had old Springfields, using powder and bullets. We used to make a shack by the edge of the woods, the others would kill the buffalo and then we would roast the meat by the fire. I used to cut the buffalo meat in strips, and dried it, and then put it in sacks and carried it along for the war party. When we made a little log shelter at night they made me stay by the door where it was cold and I had to do all the cooking for the party. We had no bucket with which to carry water, so when we killed a buffalo we took the tripe and used that for a pail in which to carry water. The scouts of the war party of course were away ahead of us and when we made our shack in the woods they would return at night. If they returned singing we knew that they had buffalo and we would run to get their packs. These scouts got up before daybreak and left the camp on another scouting expedition—they were looking for the enemy to see which way they were moving or what they had been killing. We found the trail by the marks of their old camps. The scouts trailed the enemy until they found the camp, then they returned howling like a wolf as they came near us, and then we knew they had found the enemy. When they approached the camp we made piles of different material and then they shook their guns at the piles and we knew that they were telling the truth, that they had seen the enemy. Then they run over the piles. Then we got ready for the night and stretched our ropes; we took our medicine and tied it on our heads. Then we all stood up in a row and they selected the bravest to take the lead to the camp of the enemy. Then these braves started on a run, first on a dog trot and then faster and faster until they got their speed, and then we endeavoured to keep up until we reached the enemy's camp. When we got within sight of the camp we would all sit in a row and take off our moccasins and put on new ones. Then we selected two men to go around to the camp and get all the horses they could capture and bring them back to our party. When these horses were caught and brought back to us we roped and mounted them bareback and rode away as fast as we could, driving the remainder of the horses they had captured. We kept on for days and nights without anything to eat or any rest. After we had reached our camp and had spent the night we painted ourselves and the best horses, mounted them, and started shooting guns in the air; then everybody knew that the war party was back. We rode through the camp on our horses. We did not expect the enemy to pursue us, because we had gone so far and so long that we knew we were out of their reach."

On the War Trail

"My first battle was on the Yellowstone River. I rode a roan horse. I was scouting under General Miles. We found the trail of the Nez Perce Indians.

We fought a battle twenty miles north of where Billings is now located. The Nez Perce chased the scouts back. Just at this time our interpreter, Bethune, had quit riding, for his horse had played out and he went on foot. Then many of the Nez Perce dismounted and began to surround Bethune and open fire on him. I thought then his life would be lost and I rode back as fast as I could ride into the midst of the fire, pulled him on the back of my horse and rode away, saving his life."

In his own words Goes-Ahead tells us how he became a scout in the United States Army: "I was a single man and I loved to go on the warpath. The chiefs announced to all the camp asking young men to go to the army officers and enlist as scouts. As I wanted to scout I obeyed the command of my chiefs. The army officers took the names of these young men. The young men whose names were not taken were turned back, but they always took my name, and that is how I came to be a scout." Goes-Ahead tells for us a most graphic story of his share in the Custer fight and his impressions of General Custer in the chapter on "The Indians' Story of the Custer Fight."

In Battle Line

THE INDIANS' STORY OF THE CUSTER FIGHT

We are thinking now of the reddest chapter in the Indian wars of the Western plains. Out amid the dirge of landscape, framed within the valley of the Little Big Horn, where that historic river winds its tortuous way through the sagebrush and cactus of Montana, a weather-beaten cross stands on a lonely hillside, surrounded by a cluster of white marble slabs, and all marking the final resting-place of the heroes of the Seventh United States Cavalry, who perished to a man, "in battle formation," with their intrepid leader, Gen. George A. Custer. "Custer's Last Battle," as chroniclers of Indian wars have designated that grim tragedy, has been written about, speculated upon, and discussed more than any other single engagement between white troops and Indians. Volumes have already been written and spoken on all sides—the controversy still goes on. The brave dead sleep on; they are bivouacked on Fame's eternal camping ground. Civilization has irrigated the valley and swept on to Western frontiers, but as though to forever write laurels for the brow of Custer—called the Murat of the American army—the white stones and the decaying crucifix of wood are surrounded by barren bluffs and a landscape so forbidding that it is a midnight of desolation. It seems to be preserved by the God of Battles as an inditement on the landscape never to be erased by any human court—lonely, solemn, desolate, bereaved of any summer flower, written all over with the purple shadows of an endless Miserere. Thirty-six years have run through the hourglass since these dreary hills and the flowing river listened to the furious speech of rifles and the warwhoop of desperate redmen. The snows have piled high the parchment of winter—a shroud for the deathless dead—whiter than the white slabs. Summer has succeeded summer, and all the June days since that day of terrific annihilation have poured their white suns upon these white milestones of the nation's destiny—the only requiem, the winds of winter, and in summer the liquid notes of the meadow lark. In all the argument and controversy that has shifted the various factors of the fight over the checkerboard of contention, the voice of the Indian has hitherto been hopelessly silent. It is historically significant, therefore, that the Indian now speaks, and the story of Custer's Last Battle, now told for the first time by all four of his scouts, and leaders of the Sioux and Cheyennes, should mark an epoch in the history of this grim battle. The Indians who tell this story were all of them members of the last Great Indian Council, and they visited the Custer Field a little over two miles from the camp of the chiefs, traversed every step of the ensanguined ground and verified their positions, recalling the tragic scenes of June 26, 1876. It matters much in reading their story to remember that all of Ouster's command were killed—every lip was sealed in death and the silence is forever unbroken. The Indian survivors are all old men: Goes-Ahead and Hairy Moccasin are each on the verge of the grave, fatally stricken by disease; Chief Two Moons, leader of the hostile Cheyennes, is a blind old man; Runs-the-Enemy, a Sioux chief, totters with age. In a near tomorrow they too will sink into silence.

The Custer Battlefield

These four scouts, faithful to the memory of Custer, together with the Sioux and Cheyenne chiefs, trudged with the writer to stand on the spot where Custer fell, and with bowed heads pay their silent tribute to the dead. The camera has recorded the scene, a last vision of the red man standing above the grave of his conquerors, a pathetic page in the last chapter of Indian warfare.

Scouts on the March

THE STORY OF WHITE-MAN-RUNS-HIM—CUSTER SCOUT

The Great Father at Washington sent representatives out to our country. The Indians met them and held a council. The Sioux were the hereditary enemies of the Crows. The head man sent by the Great Father said to the Crows: "We must get together and fight, and get this land from the Sioux. We must win it by conquest." We called the officer, who was lame, No-Hip-Bone— the officer was General Terry. We loved our land so we consented to go in with the soldiers and put these other tribes off the land. No-Hip-Bone took me in the winter time, and I went with him wherever he wanted me to go until the next summer. During this journey I had a good horse. The Sioux took it away from me, and I was left to go on foot, so I put my gun on my shoulder and marched with the soldiers. I thought that I was a man, and had confidence in myself that I was right. And so I kept up with the soldiers. I endured all the hardships the soldiers endured in order to hold my land. We had hardships climbing mountains, fording rivers, frost and cold of winter, the burning heat of summer—my bones ache to-day from the exposure, but it was all for love of my home. I stood faithfully by the soldiers. They did not know the country. I did. They wanted me for their eye, they could not see. The soldiers were the same as though they were blind, and I used both of my own eyes for them. The soldiers and I were fighting in friendship, what they said, I did; what I said, they did. So I helped my tribe. Land is a very valuable thing, and especially our land. I knew the Cheyennes and Sioux wanted to take it by conquest, so I stayed with the soldiers to help hold it. No-Hip-Bone moved to Tongue River at the time the leaves were getting full. We heard that General Custer was coming and I and thirty soldiers went down the river in boats. Two scouts, Elk and Two-Whistles, were with me. At the junction of the Yellowstone with the Missouri River we met Custer. I was the first one of the Crows to shake hands with General Custer. He gripped me by the hand tight and said: "You are the one I want to see, and I am glad that you are first." We went into the steamboat with General Custer, and he pointed out different places to me as objects of interest. I directed Custer up to No-Hip-Bone, who had moved to the mouth of the Little Rosebud. They had a council, Bonnie Bravo was their interpreter. General Custer said to the interpreter, pointing to me: "This is the kind of man we want for this campaign, and I want some others also." Goes-Ahead, Hairy Moccasin, White Swan, Paints-His-Face-Yellow, and Curly were chosen. There were six of us altogether. The others were sent back. We always moved ahead of Custer—we were his pilots. We always travelled at night, climbing the mountains and wading the rivers. During the day we made a concealed camp. We travelled in this way several days before we reached the Sioux camp. When we reached the top of the Wolf Mountains we saw the enemy's camp near where the Custer Field is at the present time. Hairy Moccasin, Goes-Ahead, Curly, and myself saw the camp. Custer had halted at the foot of a mountain, and we all went back and told Custer that we had seen a big camp, and it was close. Custer was rejoiced and anxious to go ahead and make the battle. The sun was just peeping when we saw the camp. It was eight or nine o'clock when we scouts all went ahead again. We got close to the place of the enemy's camp, and Custer divided the scouts, sent some across the river, and the others remained on the hill. In the meantime Custer had divided his command. Yellow Face and White Swan went with Reno across the river;

Goes-Ahead, Hairy Moccasin, Curly, and myself remained with Custer. Custer sent me to a high knoll. He said: "Go and look for me and see where I can make a success." He left it to me. When I was up there I looked around and the troops were very close upon me, and I motioned to them to come on, and we passed up on to the ridge. The Indian scouts stood in front of Custer and led his men. We went down to the Little Horn until we came to a little coulee, and were moving towards the enemy's camp. We wanted to cross the river at that place. The Sioux fired at us. We then went up the hill to the ridge. I was all along the ridge where the fight was raging. We looked over the river, and saw Reno in his engagement with the Sioux. Finally they wiped out Reno, and he retreated to the hills. Custer and all of us got off our horses here. At that time the enemy was surrounding us. They were banging away at us. We had a heavy skirmish. Custer then came up and said: "You have done your duty. You have led me to the enemy's camp. And now the thing for you to do is to obey my orders and get away." Farther on up the river was a packtrain, escorted by three hundred soldiers, and I made my way to the pack-train, and I found the Indians there fighting. Custer when he told me to go said: "You go; I am now going with my boys." Had Custer not ordered me to go, the people who visit the Custer Field to-day would see my name on the monument. When I got back to the packtrain, I directed them back to where the old trenches are to-day, and where you may still see a pile of bones. The Indians had killed all the mules when I got there. The fight lasted through the whole of a long, hot summer day. My friends, the soldiers who were with Custer, were all wiped out. When the sun went down I was about exhausted and I had no clothes on save a breechclout. All the scouts were dressed like myself. When night came on, exhausted as we were, we scouts went down the river to meet No-Hip-Bone. We reached him early the next morning. There was a terrific rainstorm all night long. I had no clothes on and I stuck to my wet horse. My horse was so exhausted that he stumbled on through the night, and to-day I feel the effects of it. It was my nature to endure; from a boy I had been trained to endure, but as strong as I was it wounded me for life. We met No-Hip-Bone and told him that up the river yesterday, when the sun was midway between morning and noon, until the sun was midway between noon and night, the Indians had killed Custer and all of his command. And he was mad. We told him that our horses' hoofs were worn out and asked permission to go back home and get fresh horses. He said: "Yes, you can go, but come back. Meanwhile I will travel up the river and see the dead soldiers." I went to Pryor, our Crow camp.

Sunset on the Custer Field

Custer and the soldiers were my friends and companions, and I cried all night long as I rode through the rain to tell No-Hip-Bone the news.

When we were at the Rosebud, General Custer and his staff held a council as to what we should do when we found the enemy's camp, as to whether we should attack by day or night. I said we had better fight by night. Paints-His-Face-Yellow said: "Let us attack by day, so that we can see what we are doing." I thought I was laying a good plan for them but they listened to Yellow-Face. General Custer was a brave and good man, a straightforward and honest man. When General Custer took me by the hand, patted me on the shoulder, and I looked him in the face, I said: "There is a good general."

If General Custer was living to-day, I would get better treatment than I now receive. General Custer said: "Where does your tribe stay?" and I told him in the valley through which Pryor Creek runs, along the Big Horn River at Lodge Grass, and in the valley of the Little Horn—there is my home. Custer said: "If I die, you will get this land back and stay there, happy and contented, and if you die, you will be buried on your own land."

When I joined General Custer, I had full confidence in myself and my ability to help him, and for this reason I joined Custer so that I might help hold my land against our enemies, the Sioux and the Cheyennes. After the Custer battle, when we had obtained fresh horses, I took the other scouts with me, and we went over the field and looked at the remains of the dead soldiers who were my friends and companions. Knowing the country I always directed General Custer to the best places to ford the river, and the easiest way to climb the hills, that he might reach the path of success. After the loss of my horse, I traveled on foot with the soldiers, and was willing even to go down to death with Custer in order that I might help him.

THE STORY OF CURLY—CUSTER SCOUT

We had been brought to the Little Rosebud down the Yellowstone by steamer. After we had landed we were told to get dinner, dress ourselves, paint up, and get ready to scout. Then we heard that General Custer wanted to use us. We mounted and rode over to General Custer's camp. He had a big tent. We got off at the door. I was the first to shake his hand. I had a dollar in my hand, and I pressed that into his hand. Each scout shook hands with him. When I saw Custer sitting there, tall and slim, with broad shoulders and kind eyes, I said to myself: "There is a kind, brave, and thinking man." The first words that Custer uttered were: "I have seen all the tribes but the Crows, and now I see them for the first time, and I think they are good and brave scouts. I have some scouts here, but they are worthless. I have heard that the Crows are good scouts, and I have sent for you to come to my command. I have given General Terry six hundred dollars for the use of you Crow Indians as scouts. I have called you Indians here not to fight but to trace the enemy and tell me where they are; I do not want you to fight. You find the Indians and I will do the fighting. With all these dollars I have given you I want you to go into the steamboat and buy some shirts and paint. We will leave here in two days. We will follow the Little Rosebud up." That evening the Mandans danced with us, and they gave us some money. Then Custer said: "I think you are good Indians. I will have the cook prepare our dinner, and you can eat alongside of me. I will have a tent put up here and you can camp near me." Within two days we started on our journey. We got on our horses and started with Custer up the Little Rosebud. The whole command were with us. He asked us where we saw the last Sioux camp while we were scouting for Terry. We told him we would not be near there until to-morrow. The next morning we were at the place where we saw the last camp of the Sioux. Then we followed the Sioux trail. We found the trail, and saw that it forked on the Little Rosebud River. Custer gave orders for Goes-Ahead to follow one trail, and for me to follow the other to see which was the largest camp. We found that the trails came together after a while and that the Sioux were all in one camp. When we got to the camp, we saw that a battle had been fought, for we found the scalps and the beards of white men. We went back that night and reported to Custer. It was pretty late, but Custer's cook was up and had a light in his tent. Then Custer told the cook to give the boys their meal. After we got through our supper we went to his tent as Custer wanted to see us. We took with us some of the scalps and white men's beards, and showed them to Custer. Then Custer asked us if the camp separated or came together, and we told him it came together. Then Custer said: "This is the main point—these Sioux have been killing white people, and I have been sent here by the Great Father to conquer them and bring them back to their reservation. I am a great chief, but I do not know whether I will get through this summer alive or dead. There will be nothing more good for the Sioux—if they massacre me, they will still suffer, and if they do not kill me, they will still suffer for they have disobeyed orders. I do not know whether I will pass through this battle or not, but if I live, I will recommend you boys and you will be leaders of the Crows. Tomorrow I want five of my Crow boys to go on the trail." We started just before daybreak. When we started we saw some of the Mandans running round on the top of the hill, and Goes-Ahead told me to go back and tell the command that they must not have these Mandans running round over the hills, but to keep them down in the valley, as we might be near the Sioux camp and would be discovered before we knew it. Then they ordered these Mandans to come down from the hills and stay down. When I started back I heard a howl like a coyote. White Swan, Hairy Moccasin, Goes-Ahead, and White-Man-Runs-Him were coming in to report. The Sioux had broken camp the day before and had camped above where their old camp was on the Little Rosebud. Custer told us to go on ahead and see which way they went, and we came to where they had broken camp. We followed the trail until we saw that they had camped on the Little Horn, and then we noticed that the Sioux had gone toward the Little Horn and we waited at the head of Tallec Creek for the command to come up. The command did not come up, for they had camped on the Little Rosebud; and we went back to the camp. Then the scouts had an argument, and I went by myself and asked Custer what we should do.

Custer asked me what I came back for. I told him that the trail of the Sioux had gone to the west, toward the Little Horn, and that I had come back for further orders. Then Custer told me to get my supper, and take a lunch for the other scouts, and take with me two soldiers and go on and camp on the hill in sight of the enemy. I was lying down at daybreak, half asleep—the boys said they saw the camp where the Sioux were located. I got up and saw them through the smoke. The command came halfway toward us and then stopped and this officer who was with us wrote a message for General Custer, and sent a Mandan scout back with it. Custer did not wait. As soon as he got the message his men moved on rapidly toward the Custer Field. Then Custer said: "We will charge upon them now—that settles their journey." Custer then gave the order to inspect their guns. Soon they started on down the ridge. Custer told us to go on ahead. We followed the creek all the way down. There was half a battalion behind us. We found a tepee like the one in which we are now sitting, as we went along, and found two dead Sioux inside. Then the main command came up to us. We all stopped at the fork of the Little Reno Creek. Custer split up his command at this point, and told Reno to follow the creek down, which is now called Reno Creek. Then we crossed over the ridge. I came down with Custer as far as the creek; then he gave me a message to take to Reno. I did not know the import of the messsage. I brought the answer back from Reno to Custer. While I was delivering the last message, Reno was fighting his battle, but it was not very fierce, and when I got to Custer with the message he was fighting at the mouth of the creek. Then Custer told me to go and save my life. I made a circle around, and I found that my ammunition was getting low. I found a dead Sioux. I took his ammunition and gun and horse, and got out. I stayed near where the dead Sioux was until the fight was pretty fierce. I went up on a high butte to the east of the battlefield where I could see the fight. When I got on the high hill I looked back, and saw that Custer was the last man to stand. After that I rushed over the hill and hid in the brush. The next morning about five or six o'clock I was at General Terry's camp and reported. General Terry called his officers about him. I could not speak English and there were no interpreters there, so I took the grass and piled it all up in a heap, then I took my fingers and scattered it wide apart, and attempted in this way to show General Terry that the soldiers were all killed. Then General Terry gave me a dispatch. I was very tired and did not want to go, but I had to take this dispatch from General Terry, to Reno at the packtrain. Reno gave me a dispatch to take back to Terry, while they were burying the dead soldiers. Then another dispatch was given me to take to the head command at the steamboat. I felt sorry and depressed that I should never again see Custer.

The Reno Battlefield

THE STORY OF GOES-AHEAD—CUSTER SCOUT

I was under General Terry at the Yellowstone at the mouth of the Big Horn. There was a boat at the mouth of the Big Horn. The steamboat had a pontoon bridge reaching to the shore. The soldiers came off the boat and joined General Terry's command. Then General Terry gave the command for us all to mount and go ahead of the line. Then he selected men from this line of scouts to send to General Custer as scouts. He mentioned my name and also called Yellow-Shield, White-Man-Runs-Him, White Swan, Hairy

Moccasin, and Curly out of this line. There were six of us. Then they gave us orders to go on the steamboat. We sailed down to the mouth of the Little Rosebud, there we got off the boat. Then our interpreter told us there was a man in the camp of the army who wanted to see us, and we went over there. Then we went into General Custer's tent; we sat on one side of the tent, and that was a day of great pleasure to me. I saw that General Custer was a man of about six feet two inches, slim and well-built, and kind-hearted. He wore long hair. General Custer told us that he had heard that the Crow Indians were the bravest scouts and the best horsemen among all the Indians, and that was the reason he asked General Terry to send us to him. He said he had some Mandan scouts but they were not going to do any Indian scouting for him, but would remain in the line and do the cooking for the scouts. Then General Custer told us he wanted us to find the Sioux trail and follow it until we reached the Sioux camp and to report to him where they were. He did not want us to enter into battle with the Sioux, but to come back and tell him the location of their camp. Then after he had won the battle he would give us all the Sioux horses we could drive home. Then we scouted in search of the Sioux. We followed the trail of the Sioux where they had been moving, and we got to where they had camped on the Little Rosebud. I got to the place where they had been camping just after their fight with General Crook at the battle of the Little Rosebud, and they had moved to the Little Horn. General Custer gave us strict orders when we were scouting not to mistake the scouts of General Terry and General Crook for the other Indians, because we might run across them and to be sure we had seen the Sioux. We were two nights on our way before we came upon the village. It was located on the plain above where the Custer fight took place, on the banks of the Little Horn. I was by myself and after I saw the village I went back and reported to General Custer and he was greatly pleased. I always tried to obey orders and follow closely my instructions. I reported to General Custer that it was a pretty big village. Custer said "That is just what I am looking for; we might just as well enter the battle." General Custer told me to go ahead of his column, and keep ahead, but not to go too far for fear the enemy would capture me, and I did what he ordered me to do. General Custer marched his troops all night up to a point about five miles from where I reported to him, and then he divided his command. Reno followed down the Reno Creek, Custer crossed the ridge, going over to the Medicine Tail Creek which runs into the Little Horn. There on the creek General Custer dismounted, and said prayers to the Heavenly Father. Then he rose and shook hands with me, and said: "My scout, if we win the battle, you will be one of the noted men of the Crow Nation." In a moment or two he turned around again and said to me: "I have forgotten to tell you, you are not to fight in this battle, but to go back and save your life." White-Man-Runs-Him and Hairy Moccasin and Curly heard what Custer said. The other two were with Reno.

We were in sight of the camp when Custer told us this. Reno had then crossed the Little Horn with his two Crow scouts and the rest of the Mandans. If we had been smart enough we would have asked General Custer to give us a paper as a recommendation, but we did not know anything much in those days. As we stood looking, we saw Reno take his battle position between eight and nine o'clock. Custer stood there a little for we expected all the Crow Creeks, and Terry's command, to meet us there that day, and make a battle that day. After he said this Custer started into the battle and opened fire on the camp. We scouts were up on top of the bluff, and we fired at the camp. Hairy Moccasin and White-Man-Runs-Him were with him. Curly I did not see because he carried the last dispatch to Reno. Although Custer had given us command to do no fighting, it was impossible for us to stand there on the bluff and see the soldiers fighting and not do something, so we had to fire. I do not want to make any mistake in this story, and I have told you the truth. Reno took the battle. There was so much smoke and dust that I could hardly tell, but Reno was driven back by the Indians toward the bluff. In all the valley and woods there was nothing but Indians. Then I did not know which way he went, for I was fighting my own way. Custer also opened fire just beyond the Medicine Creek where he had crossed. Soon after Reno opened fire Custer began his fire. From there I cannot tell you. About four or five o'clock the packtrain came up and the hard fighting was down there. I went back to the packtrain and helped fight a while and then I took to the pine hills away over to the east. When I heard that Custer had been killed I said: "He is a man to fight the enemy. He loved to fight, but if he fights and is killed, he will have to be killed."

THE STORY OF CHIEF RED CLOUD——OGOLLALA SIOUX

I remember that our camp was located in the valley of the Little Big Horn. As I remember there were about four thousand Indians in our camp, and about a hundred Sioux warriors in my own band. There were four or five different sections of the Sioux tribe in this fight. I remember that Rain-in-the-Face and Sitting-Bull, Crazy Horse, and Big Man were with us in the battle. We were in our camp; there was plenty of buffalo meat in those days, and we killed a good many. The women were drying the meat, and the warriors were resting. Suddenly we heard firing, and we found out that the soldiers were on us. The women and children were all frightened, and started to run across the hills, and we men mounted our horses and started toward the enemy. I remember that we pushed Reno back until he had to cross the river, and go up against the bluffs, and then some of our Sioux rode around the hill to head him off, and we had him in a pocket. After we had killed many of Reno's men, Custer came along the ridge, and we were called off to fight Custer. We kept circling around Custer, and as his men came down the ridge we shot them down. And then the rest dismounted and gathered in a bunch, kneeling down and shooting from behind their horses. We circled round and round, firing into Custer's men until the last man was killed. I did not see Custer fall, for all the Indians did not know which was Custer. One reason why we did not scalp Custer was because the Indians and the white soldiers were so mixed up that it was hard to distinguish one man from another; and another reason was because Custer was the bravest man of all and we did not want to touch him as he made the last stand. This is also the opinion of Rain-in-the-Face. Regarding the cause of the Custer fight I must say, we were pursued by the soldiers, we were on the warpath, and we were on the warpath with the Crows and other tribes. We were trying to drive them back from the hunting grounds, and the soldiers came upon us and we had to defend ourselves. We were driven out of the Black Hills by the men seeking gold, and our game was driven off, and we started on our journey in search of game. Our children were starving, and we had to have something to eat. There was buffalo in that region and we were moving, simply camping here and there and fighting our Indian enemies as we advanced, in order to get the game that was in this country. We fought this battle from daylight up until three o'clock in the afternoon, and all of the white men were killed. I think that Custer was a very brave man to fight all these Indians with his few men from daylight until the sun was almost going down.

THE STORY OF CHIEF RUNS-THE-ENEMY—SIOUX LEADER

I fought at the Custer fight with a band of one hundred and thirty Two-Cattle Sioux under me. With the bravery and success I had had in former battles, I was able to command the force at this fight. We were encamped for two days in the valley of the Little Big Horn. The third day we were going to break camp and move farther along, but the old men went through the camp saying they were going to stay there still another day. After the cry had gone through the camp that we were to remain, the horses were all turned loose and were feeding on the hills north and west and south, and we were resting in the camp. Everything was quiet. I went over to the big tepee where there were several leading men, and we were sitting there talking and smoking. About ten o'clock a band of Sioux, who had been visiting the camp and had gone home, came rushing back with the tidings that the soldiers were coming. We could hardly believe that the soldiers were so near, and we were not very much depressed because of the report for two reasons: the soldiers had gone back to Wyoming, and we did not think they were near enough to attack us;

and from the history of all our tribe, away back for generations, it had never been known that soldiers or Indians had attacked a Sioux camp in the daytime; they had always waited for night to come. And still we sat there smoking. In a short time we heard the report of rifles, and bullets whizzed through the camp from the other side of the river. I left my pipe and ran as hard as I could, as did all the others, to our tents. As I ran to my tent there was a scream ran through the camp: "The soldiers are here! The soldiers are here!" The Indians who were herding the horses on the hill rushed to the camp with the horses, and the dust raised just like smoke. When I got to my tent the men who were herding the horses had got the horses there, and they were screaming. I grabbed my gun and cartridge belt, and the noise and confusion was so great that we did not know what we were doing. The women were running to the hills, and my heart was mad. The guns were still firing in the upper part of the camp. I did not have time to put on my war-bonnet; I jumped on the horse I had and made a pull for where the firing was. The first thing I saw when I got to'the battle line was a horse with a bridle on with the lines hanging down, and a dead Sioux. When I got to this line of battle—I thought I was quick, but I found a lot of Sioux already there—they were rushing on up the hill. We were all naked, and the soldiers with their pack saddles and their uniforms on and their black horses looked like great big buffalo. The Sioux were all riding up the hill. We saw one lone Indian on the hill going down toward the soldiers, and the river. We could not see him as he came down the hill, but we could see the smoke coming from under his horse's head, and we all thought that he was going to make a charge on the soldiers, and we all charged. It seemed as though that one Indian had the attention of all the soldiers, and they were all firing at him. When we saw that the smoke was all going toward the soldiers that gave us a chance to charge from this side, and we all made a rush. When we made the charge we got them all stampeded. For smoke and dust we could not see the soldiers as they retreated toward the river. The Sioux were fresh, and we soon caught up with them. We passed a black man in a soldier's uniform and we had him. He turned on his horse and shot an Indian right through the heart. Then the Indians fired at this one man, and riddled his horse with bullets. His horse fell over on his back, and the black man could not get up. I saw him as I rode by. I afterward saw him lying there dead. We fought them until they rolled and tumbled and finally had to go into the river, which was very deep. We made them cross the river. The country around the river in those days was very heavily wooded. We chased some of the soldiers into the woods, and others across the river and up the hill. I did not know the name of the commander of the soldiers at that time, but I afterward heard that it was Reno. I also heard afterward that they had a big trial and charged him with being a coward, but I praised him for rushing into the camp. The reason I praised him was that he only had a few soldiers and our camp was a great camp, and he came rushing into the camp with his few soldiers. In all the history of my great-grandfather I have never known of such an attack in daylight. After they retreated over the hills and we had killed a large number of them that battle was ended. I was at the Custer Battlefield this morning, and I noticed there were no monuments up for the soldiers who fell on the Reno Field. As we had finished with the Reno battle and were returning to camp we saw two men on the Reno Hills waving two blankets as hard as they could. Two of us rode over to where they were, and they yelled to us that the genuine stuff was coming, and they were going to get our women and children. I went over with the others and peeped over the hills and saw the soldiers advancing. As I looked along the line of the ridge they seemed to fill the whole hill. It looked as if there were thousands of them, and I thought we would surely be beaten. As I returned I saw hundreds of Sioux. I looked into their eyes and they looked different—they were filled with fear. I then called my own band together, and I took off the ribbons from my hair, also my shirt and pants, and threw them away, saving nothing but my belt of cartridges and gun. I thought most of the Sioux will fall to-day: I will fall with them. Just at that time Sitting-Bull made his appearance. He said, just as though I could hear him at this moment: "A bird, when it is on its nest, spreads its wings to cover the nest and eggs and protect them. It cannot use its wings for defense, but it can cackle and try to drive away the enemy. We are here to protect our wives and children, and we must not let the soldiers get them." He was on a buckskin horse, and he rode from one end of the line to the other, calling out: "Make a brave fight!" We were all hidden along the ridge of hills. While Sitting-Bull was telling this I looked up and saw that the Cheyennes had made a circle around Custer on the west, north, and east sides, and that left a gap on the south side for us to fill. We then filled up the gap, and as we did so we looked over to the Cheyenne side, and there was a woman among the Cheyennes who was nearest the soldiers trying to fight them. While Custer was all surrounded, there had been no firing from either side. The Sioux then made a charge from the rear side, shooting into the men, and the shooting frightened the horses so that they rushed upon the ridge and many horses were shot. The return fire was so strong that the Sioux had to retreat back over the hill again. I left my men there and told them to hold that position and then I rushed around the hills and came up to the north end of the field near where the monument now stands. And I saw hundreds and hundreds of Indians in the coulees all around. The Indians dismounted and tied their horses in a bunch and got down into the coulees, shooting at the soldiers from all sides. From the point that juts out just below where the monument stands about thirty of us got through the line, firing as we went, and captured a lot of Custer's horses and drove them down to the river. The horses were so thirsty that the moment we reached the river they just stood and drank and drank, and that gave us a chance to get off our horses and catch hold of the bridles. They were all loaded with shells and blankets and everything that the soldiers carried with them. Just then I returned to my men, and the soldiers were still on the hill fighting, with some of their horses near them. Just as I got back some of the soldiers made a rush down the ravine toward the river, and a great roll of smoke seemed to go down the ravine. This retreat of the soldiers down the ravine was met by the advance of the Indians from the river, and all who were not killed came back again to the hill. After the soldiers got back from the hills they made a stand all in a bunch. Another charge was made and they retreated along the line of the ridge; it looked like a stampede of buffalo. On this retreat along the ridge, the soldiers were met by my band of Indians as well as other Sioux. The soldiers now broke the line and divided, some of them going down the eastern slope of the hill, and some of them going down to the river. The others came back to where the final stand was made on the hill, but they were few in number then. The soldiers then gathered in a group, where the monument now stands—I visited the monument to-day and confirmed my memory of it—and then the soldiers and Indians were all mixed up. You could not tell one from the other. In this final charge I took part and when the last soldier was killed the smoke rolled up like a mountain above our heads, and the soldiers were piled one on top of another, dead, and here and there an Indian among the soldiers. We were so excited during the battle that we killed our own Indians. I saw one that had been hit across the head with a war axe, and others had been hit with arrows. After we were done, we went back to the camp. After the onslaught I did not see any soldiers scalped, but I saw the Indians piling up their clothes, and there was shooting all over the hill, for the Indians were looking for the wounded soldiers and were shooting them dead. Just as I got back to the camp I heard that a packtrain was coming from over the hills. I looked over the hills and saw the Sioux and Cheyennes moving that way. I remained a little while to look after my wife and children. After I had located my family I fired off my shells and got a new supply of ammunition and went toward the packtrain. When I got over there the fighting had begun. The packtrain had already fortified itself by making entrenchments. The Indians were on the outside firing into it, and the soldiers inside were firing at the Indians. During this last fight the sun was getting low. After it grew dark the firing continued; you would see the flash of the guns in the entrenchments. The Indians would crawl up and fire a flock of arrows into the entrenchments and then scatter away. This kept up all night. I did not stay, but went home. The next morning I went over there and found that the Indians still had the packtrain surrounded and the fight was still going on. We kept at long range and continued our firing. The soldiers were all sharpshooters, and the moment we put our heads up they fired at us and nearly hit us. The news went around among all the Indians that they were to stay there, and that all the soldiers in the entrenchment would be so dry soon that they would have to get out and we would get them. I cannot quite remember, but I think it was about noon—we held them until then—when news came from our camp down on the plain that there was a big bunch of soldiers coming up the river—General Terry with his men. As soon as we heard this we let the packtrain go and fled back to our camp. We at once broke camp and fled up the Little Big Horn, or Greasy Creek, as it is called by the Indians. If it had not been for General Terry coming up as he did we would have had that packtrain, for they were all dry—they had had no water for two days. After we had killed Custer and all his men I did not think very much about it. The soldiers fired into us first and we returned the fire. Sitting-Bull had talked to us and all the tribes to make a brave fight and we made it. When we had killed all the soldiers we felt that we had done our duty, and felt that it was a great battle and not a massacre. With reference to the real reason for this fight I may say that the talk among the Indians was that they were going to compel us to stay on the reservation and take away from us our country. Our purpose was to move north and go as far north as possible away from the tribes. Our object was not to fight the Crows or any other tribe, but we learned that the soldiers were getting after us to try to compel us to go back on the reservation, and we were trying to get away from them. During the Custer fight our tents were not attacked, but after the battle the women gathered up their dead husbands and brothers, and laid them out nicely in the tepee, and left them. I understand that after we had left the tepees standing, holding our dead, the soldiers came and burned the tepees. According to my estimate there were about two thousand able-bodied warriors engaged in this fight; they were all in good fighting order. The guns and ammunition that we gathered from the dead soldiers of Custer's command put us in better fighting condition than ever before, but the sentiment ran around among the Indians that we had killed enough, and we did not want to fight any more. There has been a good deal of dispute about the number of Indians killed. About the closest estimate that we can make is that fifty Sioux were killed in the fight, and others died a short time afterward from their wounds.

Two Moons as he fought Custer

THE STORY OF CHIEF TWO MOONS—CHEYENNE LEADER, AS TOLD WHERE CUSTER FELL

It was a September day. The hoarfrost had written the alphabet of the coming winter—there was promise of snow. With Chief Two Moons and his interpreter we climbed the dreary slopes leading to the monument and graves of the Custer dead. Chief Two Moons took his position by the stone which reads: "Brevet Major General George A. Custer, 7th U. S. Cavalry, fell here June 26th, 1876." A tiny flag waved by this stone, marking the spot where the hero made his last stand. The hills all about us wore a sombre hue; the sky kept marriage bonds with the scene. Cold, gray clouds hung over the ridges along which Custer rode with the daring Seventh. They draped the summits of the Big Horn Range on the far horizon in gray and purple. The prairie grass had come to the death of the autumn and it too creaked amid the stones. The heart beat quick at the sight of Chief Two Moons, a tall and stalwart Roman-faced Indian, standing amid the white slabs where thirty-three years before, clad in a white shirt, red leggings, without war-bonnet, he had ridden a white horse, dealing deathblows to the boys in blue, and with these deathblows the last great stand of the Red Man against the White Man. The battle echoes are heard again as Two Moons tells his story:

"Custer came up along the ridge and across the mountains from the right of the monument. The Cheyennes and the Sioux came up the coulee from the foot of Reno Hill, and circled about. I led the Cheyennes as we came up. Custer marched up from behind the ridge on which his monument now stands, and deployed his soldiers along the entire line of the ridge. They rode over beyond where the monument stands down into the valley until we could not see them. The Cheyennes and the Sioux came up to the right over in the valley of the Little Big Horn. Custer placed his men in groups along this ridge. They dismounted. The men who had dismounted along the ridge seemed to have let their horses go down the other side of the ridge. Those who were on the hill where the monument now stands, and where I am now standing, had gray horses and they were all in the open. The Sioux and the Cheyennes came up the valley swarming like ants toward the bunch of gray horses where Long Hair stood. I led the Cheyennes up the long line of ridge from the valley blocking the soldiers, and I called to my Cheyenne brothers: 'Come on, children; do not be scared!' And they came after me, yelling and firing. We broke the line of soldiers and went over the ridge. Another band of Indians and Sioux came from over beyond the ridge, and when I got over there, I got off my white horse and told my men to wait, and we loaded our guns and fired into the first troop which was very near us. At the first volley the troop at which we fired were all killed. We kept firing along the ridge on which the troops were stationed and kept advancing. I rode my horse back along the ridge again and called upon my children to come on after me. Many of my Cheyenne brothers were killed, and I whipped up my horse and told them to come on, that this was the last day they would ever see their chief, and I again started for the bunch of gray horses on the hilltop. The Indians followed me, yelling and firing. I could not break the line at the bunch of gray horses and I wheeled and went to the left down the valley with the line of soldiers facing me as I went, firing at me, and all my men firing at the soldiers. Then I rode on up the ridge to the left. I met an Indian with a big war-bonnet on, and right there I saw a soldier wounded. I killed him and jumped off my horse and scalped him. The Indian I met was Black Bear, a Cheyenne. I then rode down the ridge and came to a group of four dead soldiers; one of them had on a red flannel shirt, the other three had red stripes on the arm, one had three stripes, the other had three stripes and a sword. They all had on good clothes, and I jumped off my horse and took their clothes and their guns. When I turned back I could not see anything but soldiers and Indians all mixed up together. You could hardly tell one from the other. As I rode along the ridge I found nearly all the soldiers killed. I again rode up to the ridge along which Custer's troops had been stationed. I found two or three killed and saw one running away to get on top of the high hills beyond, and we took after him, and killed him."

"The whole valley was filled with smoke and the bullets flew all about us, making a noise like bees. We could hardly hear anything for the noise of guns. When the guns were firing, the Sioux and Cheyennes and soldiers, one falling one way and one falling another, together with the noise of the guns, I shall never forget. At last we saw that Custer and his men were grouped on the side of the hill, and we commenced to circle round and round, the Sioux and the Cheyennes, and we all poured in on Custer and his men, firing into them until the last man was shot. We then jumped off our horses, took their guns, and scalped them."

"After the fight was over we gathered in the river bottom and cut willow sticks, then some Indians were delegated to go and throw down a stick wherever they found a dead soldier, and then they were ordered to pick up the sticks again, and in this way we counted the number of dead. It was about six times we had to cut willow sticks, because we kept finding men all along the ridge. We counted four hundred and eighty-eight with our sticks along the ridge. We were trying to count the dead there in the valley when General Terry came up from the other side, and we fled away. After the battle was over the Indians made a circle all over the ridges and around through the valley to see if they could find any more soldiers, as they were determined to kill every one. The next morning after the fight we went up behind the Reno Field and camped at Black Lodge River. We then followed the Black Lodge River until we came back to the Little Big Horn again. Then we camped at the Little Big Horn, moving our camp constantly, fearing pursuit by the soldiers."

"Before the Custer fight we went over on the Tongue River and found a camp of soldiers. We rushed upon them and took all their horses away, and the soldiers ran into the brush. We knew there would be other soldiers after us; we knew about where they were, and we felt they would pursue us. At Powder River the soldiers attacked our camp and destroyed everything, and that made us mad. When the soldiers came after us, on the day of the Custer fight, we were ready to kill them all. The soldiers were after us all the time, and we had to fight."

The lonely stretches of prairie, the lonelier graves, the pathetic remnant of Red Men—victors on this field—the hollow silence of these dreary hill slopes, the imperishable valour of two hundred and seventy-seven men who laid their lives on a blood-red altar, until the one lone figure of the great captain lifted his unavailing sword against a howling horde of savage warriors—glittering for a moment in the June sunlight, then falling to the earth baptized with blood—is the solemn picture to forever hang in the nation's gallery of battles.

CONCLUSIONS

Fair play is an all compelling creed. Justice to the dead is one of the commandments in that creed. Let the controversy rage. Let the sword be unsheathed in the face of misrepresentation and wrong. General Custer was a daring and chivalrous officer. He had won laurels on many a hard fought field under Southern skies—he was a strategist, brave and unfaltering. He had served in Western campaigns with distinction and success. He knew how to deal with the masterful generalship of his wily Indian foes. Hitherto his tactics had been victorious. The orders under which he now marched to battle were definite up to a certain point—then, so the record in the War Department reads—he was to use his own discretion and initiative. He was compelled to follow this course—for he marched over a wild and trackless waste, far distant from his base of supplies and absolutely without means of communication with headquarters, and without ability to ascertain the movements of any military force in the field. It is fair to state that the ranking General in charge of this campaign against the Indians reposed this confidence in General Custer, otherwise, knowing the Indian as a fighter, knowing the character of the desolated wastes of country to traverse—the difficulties to be encountered in the simple movement of troops—the annihilation of any body of troops, when once they reached the unmapped plains cut in twain by gorges and piled high with impassable buttes, he would have stultified himself had not orders been given allowing discretion at the moment of emergency. Custer was strong enough, brave enough, and sufficiently masterful to see and seize the situation. His tactics were the tactics he had previously and many times employed, and always with brilliant success. On this June day he would have led the daring "Seventh" to victory and routed, if not conquered, the great Indian camp. He was defeated and slain with his entire command. They fell at their posts in battle formation. Why? The entire group of Indian warriors participating in this grim battle all testify that had Reno pushed his charge when first he attacked the Indian camp that they would have fled in confusion, for the attack was unexpected.

The Indian always expected a night attack. They further testify that after Reno made his attack with a portion of his men, thus depleting his effective fighting force by one half and in desperation made his bungling retreat, had he later come to the aid of Custer with the added reinforcements of Benteen, French, and Weir, who begged him to hear the appeal of Custer's rapid volleys, Custer would have broken the Indian camp. Reno remained on the hill until every gun was silent. Reno failed. Custer was slain. This conclusion is the voice of the Indian.

THE LAST GREAT INDIAN COUNCIL

Kabibonok Ka, the North Wind, came marching out of the caverns and snows of the north, whipping and driving blinding gusts of rain and sleet. Nee-ba-naw baigs, the Water Spirits, unsealed their fountains, and the turbulent waters of the Little Big Horn River rushed on, tearing out the banks along which on the plain were huddled the myriad tepees of the Indian camp. The wind in the trees roared like distant thunder. The dogs were crouching in any shelter. Horses were standing with their backs to the storm, their tails drenched and driven between their legs. The flaps of the tepees were closed, and the rawhide streamers from the poles cracked like the sharp report of a rifle. The women and children were closely huddled around the lodge fire. It was the great spring storm, the last triumphant blast of winter. Yonder in the centre of all this dripping circle of tepees stood the council lodge. Inside were gathered the great chief and his medicine men and warriors. They encircled the blazing logs, heeding little the melancholy night that kept tune with the sorrowful thoughts of their own hearts. The ashes had cooled in the bowl of the council pipe, when, at the head of the circle, Chief Plenty Coups, chief of all the Crow Nation, arose from his blankets, laid down his coup stick, and addressed his brothers:

"The ground on which we stand is sacred ground. It is the dust and blood of our ancestors. On these plains the Great White Father at Washington sent his soldiers armed with long knives and rifles to slay the Indian. Many of them sleep on yonder hill where Pahaska—White Chief of the Long Hair—so bravely fought and fell. A few more passing suns will see us here no more, and our dust and bones will mingle with these same prairies. I see as in a vision the dying spark of our council fires, the ashes cold and white. I see no longer the curling smoke rising from our lodge poles. I hear no longer the songs of the women as they prepare the meal. The antelope have gone; the buffalo wallows are empty. Only the wail of the coyote is heard. The white man's medicine is stronger than ours; his iron horse rushes over the buffalo trail. He talks to us through his 'whispering spirit.' " (The Indian's name for the telegraph and telephone.) "We are like birds with a broken wing. My heart is cold within me. My eyes are growing dim—I am old. Before our red brothers pass on to the happy hunting ground let us bury the tomahawk. Let us break our arrows. Let us wash off our war paint in the river. And I will instruct our medicine men to tell the women to prepare a great council lodge. I will send our hunters into the hills and pines for deer. I will send my runners to the lodges of the Blackfeet, where in that far north flowers border the snow on the hills. I will send them across the fiery desert to the lodges of the Apaches in the south. I will send them east to the lodges of the Sioux, warriors who have met us in many a hard battle. I will send them to the west, where among the mountains dwell the Cayuse and the Umatillas. I will have the outliers build smoke signals on all the high hills, calling the chiefs of all the tribes together, that we may meet here as brothers and friends in one great last council, that we may eat our bread and meat together, and smoke the council pipe, and say farewell as brothers, never to meet again." The storm abated. The urn of the morning seemed overturned, and the spices of a new spring day, redolent with the perfume of growing things, bright with sunshine and song of birds, flowed over the busy Indian camp. Weeks passed on. Runners came into camp, rushing into the lodge of the great chief, announcing the approach of a procession of chiefs from the north; other heralds told of a great company on the hills coming from the east, and from the west, and warrior chiefs from the south halted outside the camp. Chiefs from all the great tribes had heard the call, had seen the smoke signal, and now the plain is full of horses and gayly coloured riders as they dismount before the council lodge.

A wonderful blaze of colour meets the eye. Excitement and interest fill the air as these veterans of the plains enter the council lodge. Chief Plenty Coups then receives the chiefs; they are greeted one by one with a courtly and graceful dignity. When the council had assembled Chief Plenty Coups laid his coup stick and pipe sack on the ground, and in the sign language gave welcome to the chiefs from many lands.

"I am glad at heart to stand here to-day on this Indian ground and give a hearty welcome to all the chiefs assembled from the various tribes from all over the United States. It is a day of beauty, and bright sunshine; it is a glad day for me. I rejoice that on this happy day we can all meet here as friends, eat our bread and meat in communion, smoke the council pipe, and the pipe of peace. I am rejoiced to give you all a great heart of welcome. And then we must say farewell, but we go away as friends, never to meet again. I am glad to have you here."

Then Chief Two Moons, the leader of the Cheyennes in the Custer fight, arose and shook hands with Chief Plenty Coups, and said:

"This is a glad day for me, and I am glad at heart that we can all meet as chiefs from the various tribes from all over the land. It is a great day for all of us, because there are no more wars between us, and we meet in peace to hold this last great council of the chiefs, and smoke the pipe of peace. I am glad at heart that this great picture is to be made of us, as we are assembled here, because our old chiefs are fast dying away, and our old Indian customs soon will pass out of sight, and the coming generations will not know anything about us, but this picture will cause us to live all through the years.

And our children and their children will reap the benefit. I am glad we are here."

Tottering with age, and nearly blind, Tin-Tin-Meet-Sa, head chief of the Umatilla Indians, pulled himself up on his walking-stick, took Chief Plenty Coups by the hand, and said:

"I have come here to-day and am glad to meet all the chiefs and especially Chief Plenty Coups, chief of the Crow tribe. And I am greatly satisfied to meet you all and be at peace. On this day we meet as Indians and as brothers, and now we sit here on this ground and smoke the peace pipe. We meet as brothers that have been away from one another for many years. Some of us have never seen each other before, and to-day we meet and shake hands with these chiefs whom we shall never see again. Although these people were our enemies at one time, to-day we are in peace, and I think very much of this chief, and I think very much of all the chiefs. I think it is a great day for all of us. I cannot give you any more words, as I am of old age."

Umapine, head chief of the Cayuse tribe, wearing perhaps the finest regalia of any chief in the council, with great dignity and grace addressed Chief Plenty Coups:

"We all chiefs of different tribes meet here in this country, the country that some of us perhaps will never see any more. I appreciate your kindness in greeting us. We all Indians are in peace toward each other as well as toward our white brothers. I am very glad to meet you all. I hope that we will in the future days respect one another, also respect our white brothers, because we all, each one of us, belong to the animal kingdom. This is all to you, my dear friends; wishing you a good health."

Red Cloud, head chief of the Ogallalla Sioux Nation, with his captivating way, addressed Chief Plenty Coups:

"I stand here to-day to shake hands with the chief of the Crow Nation, and all the chiefs of the tribes assembled from the various quarters of our country. I stand here on this great plain, with the broad sunlight pouring down upon it. I want you to look me in the face, and I hope the Great Heavenly Father, who will look down upon us, will give all the tribes His blessing, that we may go forth in peace, and live in peace all our days, and that He will look down upon our children and finally lift us far above this earth; and that our Heavenly Father will look upon our children as His children, that all the tribes may be His children, and as we shake hands to-day upon this broad plain, we may forever live in peace. We have assembled here to-day as chiefs from all over the land; we eat the bread and meat together, we smoke the pipe of peace, and we shake the hand of peace. And now we go out as one chief, and I hope we shall be as brothers and friends for all our lives, and separate with kind hearts. I am glad to-day as I shake hands with my brothers and friends, although I shall never see them again. When the white man first came across the ocean, the Indian took him by the hand and gave him welcome. This day makes me think of that time, and now I say farewell."

Mountain Chief, head chief of the Blackfoot Indians, perhaps the most vigorous talker in the sign language in the council, greeted Chief Plenty Coups with these words:

"I have come clear across the plains and from behind the distant mountains to meet these chiefs assembled in council, and I am very glad that I am here to see these Indian chiefs from all the various tribes, and my heart is open to you all as to my own brother. We smoke the pipe of peace and take the hand of all the different chiefs, and I shall be glad forever, and shall look upon this as one of the greatest days of my life. We separate from each other in peace, and with a kind heart, but never to meet again."

Bear Ghost, Chief of the Yankton Sioux, with great calmness and deliberation said:

"I am glad that I am here to shake the hand in peace with all the chiefs of the various tribes assembled. It is a great day for me, and a great day for us all. I rejoice that a record is to be made of this council that it may live for future generations. I am glad that I can smoke the pipe of peace, and that with a sad but satisfied heart I can say farewell to all the chiefs."

The commanding figure of Koon-Kah-Za-Chy, an eminent Apache chief, stood before Chief Plenty Coups compelling the attention of the entire council: "As I stand before you to-day my mind runs over the many fierce battles that my own tribe, the Apaches, have had with the Kiowas, Cheyennes, Sioux, and other tribes. Many of the chiefs present to-day I have met before on the battlefield, but my heart is glad as I shake hands with all the chiefs to know that now we are all at peace. We smoke the pipe of peace. We meet as friends and brothers. I am glad to meet all these chiefs before I die, in peace, as I have before met them in war. It is a great day for me, for I have come far across the plains of the south, and I shall go back home carrying with me the memory of this council, and of these chiefs whom I shall never see again. I say farewell!"

Curly, Custer scout, advanced with great readiness and ease, and took the hand of Chief Plenty Coups. According to the custom of the Crows he did not lay down his coup stick, but gestured with one hand. He said:

"Dear Brother Plenty Coups, I am here to-day to greet you, and to greet all these other chiefs, chiefs who were once my enemies. My heart goes out to that great battlefield and that great monument erected to my dear Custer, with whom, and for whom, I fought. He fell on yonder hilltop almost within reach of our arms from this council lodge. And my heart is glad that I can shake hands with these chiefs, some of whom I fought against with Custer on that great battlefield. I have pledged myself never to lay aside this coup stick so long as the blood runs through my fingers, but I have resolved this day, as I look into the faces of these great chiefs who were once my enemies, that I will never lift the coup stick again, that I will live as a brother to all the tribes, and at peace with all men. I say farewell to the chiefs, a last, sad farewell."

After these and other eminent chiefs had made reply to the address of welcome given by Chief Plenty Coups, according to Indian custom they were all seated in rows on the ground in semicircles, the more eminent chiefs in the first row, the lines falling back until they reached the wall line of the lodge. Every chief wore his full war regalia and carried with him all of his ceremonial and sacred insignia. The small army of coup sticks, always held aloft, presented a suggestive picture, for these coup sticks of the many chiefs from many lands each told a story of struggle and achievement, but in the speeches made by the chiefs each coup stick was to become a pledge of peace.

Now, following the ancient custom, while still seated, an Indian woman belonging to the Blackfoot tribe and wearing the full costume of her people, together with two Cheyenne maidens, dressed in the costume of their particular tribe, entered the council lodge carrying wooden bowls filled with meat and bread. This they served to the chiefs with a wooden fork. This to them answered as a ceremony of communion. When all had partaken, Chief Plenty Coups took the two long-stemmed pipes with red sandstone bowls containing emblematic decorations the whole length of the stems—pipes that had been filled by the medicine men and placed on the ground before the standing place of the great chiefs in the centre of the lodge. Chief Plenty Coups then lighted one pipe and passed it to the chiefs at his left, and lighting the other he smoked it himself for the first, and then passed it on to the right, each chief in turn smoking the pipe, then passing it on to his brother chief, until all had smoked the council pipe. When the pipes were returned to Chief Plenty Coups they were again filled and lighted, smoked by the Great Chief, and passed on to the others. And this became the Pipe of Peace.

These Indian councils were the legislative halls of the tribes; thither all matters of importance were brought by the chiefs and the warriors. Here all tribal problems were discussed. Here the destiny of any particular tribe was settled. Here the decision to make war was reached. In these council lodges, around the blazing fire, the Indians have uttered speech more eloquent than a Pitt or a Chatham in St. Stephens or a Webster in a Senate hall, an oratory that aroused the disintegrated Indian tribes and far separated clans into such a masterful and resistful force that the Indian against odds many times mightier than himself has been able to withstand the aggressions of civilization.

When questions of such moment made the necessity, chiefs of all the tribes attended and entered into solemn council. Then the council meant war. The day finally dawned when the Indian as a race was conquered by the white man. The ranks of the chiefs became thinner and thinner until in this day only a few of the great warriors remain. These representatives of former greatness and prowess gathered from their peaceful wigwams from many and faraway lands to hold once again and for the last time a council of the old days. On this day the council was for peace, and the dominant, resonant note ringing through every sentiment uttered; if we did not know they were Indians and did not know that this was an Indian council, we would have said this was a Peace Conference at The Hague.

To stand in the presence of these mighty men of the plains, to witness their nobility, to listen to their eloquence, to think with them the mighty thoughts of their dead past, to watch their solemn faces, to tremble before the dignity of their masterful bearing, to cherish the thought of all that they have been and all that they might have been, to realize that as their footfalls leave this council lodge they have turned their backs on each other forever, and that as they mount their horses and ride away to their distant lodges they are riding into the sunset and are finally lost in the purple mists of evening, is to make the coldest page of history burn with an altar fire that shall never go out.

The Council Pipe

INDIAN IMPRESSIONS OF THE LAST GREAT COUNCIL

To the student of Indian affairs it might at first seem that the gathering of the great chiefs from all the Indian tribes, wearing war-shirt and war-bonnet, carrying their coup sticks, tomahawks, spears, bows and arrows, guns and tom-toms, would necessarily reemphasize to the Indian the glory of his former prestige, and this impression would gather such momentum that deleterious results would follow; but an alert and studious effort was always manifest to inculcate in the Indian mind that this last great council of the chiefs had for its dominant idea the welfare of the Indian, that he should live at peace with his fellows and all men, and the making of a lasting historic record of the fast-fading manners and customs of the North American Indian. This paramount idea gained such fast hold of the Indian mind that the council became not only a place of historic record but a school for the inculcation of the highest ideals of peace. That the lesson was well taught and well learned becomes strikingly evident in the peace sentiments of the chiefs expressed in their speeches at the council, and their impressions of the council now to follow:

Chief Plenty Coups Addressing the Council

CHIEF PLENTY COUPS: I have a very glad heart to-day because it has been my privilege to welcome the chiefs from all the great tribes, all over the United States, here on these beautiful plains of Montana. I am rejoiced that on this day of beauty and bright sunshine we could meet together. I am glad to welcome as my guests Indian chiefs whom I have never seen, and that I could give them a welcome with my heart open, eat with them bread and meat, and smoke the pipe of peace, and greet all the chiefs as brothers. As the bright sun has opened upon us, Doctor Dixon has met us all in peace and friendliness and we all feel toward him with a kind heart. His coming has brought about the coming of the chiefs whom I have never seen before and will never see again, and as the chief of the Crow Nation I am rejoiced to give him and all these chiefs a great heart of welcome, and send them away in peace, and I feel that they are all like my own brothers. During my life from my early days I have fought the other nations before the white man ever stepped into this country, then the Great Father ordered that we should stop fighting and live in peace. Before this we conquered each other's horses and killed on all sides. And now to-day we have met in this great council as chiefs and friends. The Great Father is good to us again in permitting us to have this meeting, and I look upon all these chiefs and all the tribes as my friends. And as the bright sunshine falls, I pray that our Heavenly Father may let His blessing come down upon all the chiefs and all the tribes, and that we may go forth from this great day happy and in peace. In former days we were in ceaseless conflict; then Uncle Sam came to us and said we must live in peace. And since that time we have had allotments of land, schools have been built for the education of our children, and as an illustration of the feelings of my heart to-day—the tribes have all met here and we have met in peace, and have met as one man. We are all as brothers—the tobacco of all the tribes is as the tobacco of one man, and we have all smoked the pipe of peace together. Out of the struggle of these old days we have come into the calm and serene light of such a day as this. This I consider to be the greatest event of my life, and my country I shall live for, and my country shall remain in peace, as I feel peaceful toward my country.

CURLY: Since my boyhood days I have never seen anything so great. We have seen here the chiefs from all over the United States. It was wonderful. You are the first man that ever brought such a thing to pass. I enjoyed it very much more than I can tell. The thought of this thing was a great thought, one of the greatest thoughts of our time. Many of our Indians have gone to Washington, and have seen the Great White Father, and have seen great things. These Indian chiefs have all been brought here so that we could see them and talk with them by the sign language, and I think it is most wonderful.

CHIEF RED WHIP: I think this is a great idea. I am glad to meet the chiefs of all the tribes. I have never seen them before. It will not be long until all these big chiefs are dead, and the younger generation will read the history of these chiefs and see these pictures, and I am glad the record is being made.

Chief Koon-Ka-Za-Chy Addressing the Council

CHIEF KOON-KAH-ZA-CHY: I never before have seen so many chiefs meet together. I have met a great many chiefs here whom I have never seen before. When I was asked to come here I heard it was for the purpose of making a record, and to me the thought was good. I am sorry in my heart that I must say farewell to all these chiefs.

CHIEF RUNNING BIRD: I am sixty years old, and when I came to this ground it was ground I had never seen before in my life. I met the chiefs whom I had never seen before. I had heard of them but had not seen them. I was very glad to come here and see the old-time tepees, the kind of tepees our fathers used to live in. I grew up to manhood myself in this kind of a tepee, and I had good health. Now When they give us a house to live in I am not healthy at all. I am getting old now, and am getting up in years, and all I wish now at the present time is that my children shall grow up industrious and work, because they cannot get honour in the war as I used to get it—they can only get honour now by working hard. I can only teach my children that the way to get honour is to go to work, and be good men and women. These impressions have been strengthened by this council. I shall go home and tell the other Indians and our agent about the council, for the meeting of the chiefs will always live in my memory.

CHIEF BRAVE BEAR: The meeting of all the chiefs, my friends and those who are strangers to me, makes my heart feel high. I think of this and when I get back I shall still think of it, and it will be just as though I was here. I will never forget these men sitting here as my friends, as long as I live. We have been treated kindly and this I shall never forget. I would like a nice little story of this meeting so that I can show it to my friends.

CHIEF UMAPINE: I have come from the far distant mountains of Oregon to meet the chiefs in council. I cannot understand their language; I can only talk to them in signs, but I have great respect for them. We each have two hands, two feet, two eyes, two ears, but one nose, one mouth, one head, and one heart. We all breathe the same air; we are all, therefore, brothers. On my journey to this land, where in former years I have chased the buffalo and fought the hostile Sioux who came to steal our horses and women, I saw the old buffalo trails where these great beasts used to march in single file, each walking in the footsteps of the other until they had worn deep their trail. The snows of many winters have cut the trail deep like an irrigating ditch, and when I thought of the buffalo I cried in my heart. I have taken these great chiefs by the hand, I have been glad to meet them; I must now say farewell forever, and my heart is more lonely than when I think of the buffalo.

CHIEF TIN-TIN-MEET-SA: My idea of this meeting is that we are doing a great thing. I am of old age and I feel strange to these people whom I have met here at this place for the first time. I know that after this meeting is over we will all of us go back to our own country, probably never to see one another again, or talk any more to each other. The man who was sent here to do this work has been very kind to the Indians and is a fit man to do this kind of work. The work he is doing is one of the greatest works that has ever been done. The record here made will not perish. We will soon all be gone, but the record will last. I have no hard feelings toward any one in this camp, and I am only worrying about my hay at home.

CHIEF PRETTY VOICE EAGLE: The meeting of the chiefs is to me a great thing in many ways. First: I was glad to come here and meet the chiefs from all over the country, and see many whom I had never seen before, and talk to them by sign language. It is a great sign to me that we have all met here, met in peace. We had this feeling before we came, but now that we are here and can see each other face to face, the feeling has grown. Second: it is a great idea that has been thought of to send a man here to take our speeches and make our pictures, and think over and talk over the old times, and make a record of them. To me this is a great accomplishment. It is a great accomplishment in this way: we cannot go to Washington; we cannot present ourselves there, but the pictures and the record will be preserved there and in great cities, to speak for us. I want to draw a little illustration. You speak a language that we know nothing about. With the help of your people you have educated the younger element and through them we can speak to you, and the different interpreters can speak for the different tribes to you, and thus we can all talk with you and tell our story. I want to point out in this way the difference between the old people and the young people. The illustration I have given seems to me like a dream. I can see the advancement our race has made thus far. Our race is constantly changing, and this meeting will be a great memory to all the Indians represented here. This meeting means a great deal to my tribe. One great feeling of gratefulness I have about this meeting is that I hope that my grandchildren and their grandchildren will read the speeches I have made here, and will see my pictures.

CHIEF RUNNING FISHER: I think there is a great idea back of calling the chiefs together, because there will be something left of us when we are all gone. This record and pictures will live when we are all dead. I am glad to have had this privilege of meeting all these chiefs from all the tribes. I feel sad at the thought of not meeting these chiefs again, for I would like to meet them all once more, but I feel pretty sure we will never meet again.

Chief Running Fisher died within two weeks after reaching home from the council.

CHIEF BULL-DON'T-FALL-DOWN: This meeting of the great chiefs in council I consider one of the great events of my life. Chiefs from all over the United States have come here, chiefs whom I have never seen before and whom I will never see again. We have had an opportunity to see their faces, shake hands with them, and talk with them in the sign language. Since the great council of the chiefs on the Platte River in 1867, we have not seen any of their faces until this day. Then we were on the warpath—at this council we meet in peace. I was one of the first Crow Indians to make peace with the Sioux after we had been on the warpath, and now I can say farewell to all the chiefs with peace in my heart for all men.

Chief Two Moons Addressing the Council

CHIEF TWO MOONS: I feel that I am engaging in a great work in helping to make this historic picture of a great Indian council. I have led the Cheyennes in so many battles, and my life has been so full, that I felt when I came here that I was an old man, but since meeting the chiefs and having a share in the great council and recalling my old life for this record, I feel like a young man again. It is a great day for all of us, because there are no more wars between us, and we meet in peace and hold this great council of the chiefs and smoke the pipe of peace. I am glad at heart that this great picture is to be made of us, as we are assembled here, because our old chiefs are fast dying away, and our old Indian customs soon will pass out of sight. This record will survive for our children, and their children will reap the benefit. I am glad we are here, but my heart is sorry to say farewell.

CHIEF RED CLOUD: I think this a great and good thing. Good things have come to us from the white man. When the white man came across the ocean we heard he was coming because there was land over here, and he brought us food to eat. The coming of this man to make these pictures, to be preserved in Washington and to be shown in great cities, means good to us, because the generations to come will know of our manners and customs. It is good, besides, to meet all these chiefs who are as brothers to one another. We have never met them before; we shall never see their faces again, and it is, therefore, I think, a great and good thing to have this last council of the chiefs.

MOUNTAIN CHIEF: I think it was one of the greatest things that ever happened when we had this great council. It will be remembered forever. As for myself, it will not be very long until I go to the happy hunting grounds, but I have left this record for the coming generations. While I was sitting in the council I was thinking of the past when we used not to see each other's faces, except with the firing of guns, and now we have met the different tribes in council to talk with one another in the sign language. It shows that the Government is greater than the Indian. I think it was a great thing to bring these chiefs together, and so long as I live I am going to tell this story to my children and my grandchildren. I think that Chief Two Moons and Chief Plenty Coups were the two greatest men in the council. They impressed me more than any others by their appearance. Two Moons was not dressed up, but he showed that he was a man. I feel as I sit talking here with you that we are brothers together. And I say farewell to all the chiefs with a sad heart.

CHIEF WHITE HORSE: This council of all the chiefs seems to me to be a wonderful idea. I have met a good many whom I have never seen before, and it was a great surprise to me, and my heart felt glad. These different tribes of Indians have been enemies to each other for generations back, but we have now been at peace with each other for many years. But now we all meet here and see each other. I think your idea of taking notes and making a record of our lives and taking pictures of us, of our Indian costumes and our manners, is a great thing. I am old enough now and do not expect to live very long, but I am very glad that this record is to be made, and put on file in the Great Father's house at Washington. Another thing I would like to say: we all speak different languages, and we are all as helpless as a child, and we want you to help us in our needs during our last days. My trip here was the first time I have ever been on an iron horse, and there are a great many lessons that I learned from my ride here. When I came here and saw all the Indians speaking different languages and looking different, and I saw all that was going on and heard their speeches by sign language, I thought it was one of the most important events in my life. The first lesson I got while riding on the iron horse was to see the coaches filled with white people, and when I went in they all looked at me and looked as though I was a great curiosity to them. When I first saw the white people I felt backward—they looked at me so hard. I felt backward, but I finally felt more at ease, for I thought, I am going to die anyway. I looked over the white people and their dress, and I looked over the ceiling of the coach, and I thought these are all wonderful things. I looked out of the window and the train was going so fast that it seemed to me I was on the wings of a great bird. We travelled so fast I could not see the things very near the coach. When we used to travel on our ponies it took us many days to come over to this place. But on the train it took us one half day to come to Miles City, and that was one of the things that made me fear. It seems impossible how the trains go so fast, and this thought came to my mind: This is of the white people, who are so educated they can make the iron horse draw things across the country so fast. My wish is that the Indians will come to be like the white people, and be able to invent things, but the thought comes to me that this will be impossible. As we came along, flying as a bird, I looked out of the window, saw a country over which I had once hunted, and the thought of the buffalo came back to me, and I cried in my heart. When I get home I expect to stay there, and never leave my country again. I shall never see this land any more. I expect to die at home. When I get home I shall tell my people of the journey I had on the train, and what I saw, and of my visit to this great country, of the speeches that we made, of the pictures that were taken, and I know when I tell them they will be glad.

An Indian Communion

The Final Trail

THE FAREWELL OF THE CHIEFS

We are standing at the centre of a mighty circumference. An Indian world revolves for the last time upon its axis. All the constellations which gave it light have burned out. The Indian cosmos sweeps a dead thing amid the growing lustre of the unfading stars of civilization and history. The solemn hour passes, unmarked by any cataclysm of nature—volcano and earthquake utter no speech—darkness and tempest rend no veil of this crumbling life temple. In the deepening twilight all is silent—all speech is vulgar. To utter a word here would be profanation. The remnant of a race have gathered for shelter within the sacred walls of their council lodge. The ashes of the council pipe have been scattered upon the ground. In silence, deep, profound, awe-inspiring, the old Indian guard—the Last of the Great Chiefs—break not the silence. Who can ask death to retreat? And who put in shackles the decrees of destiny? The world annals contain no heroism and no bravery more lofty and enduring than that furnished by the record of the red man. But the summital requirement is at hand. These old heroes, few in number, must with their own moccasined feet measure the distance in yards and inches from that council lodge to the grave—the grave of their race. It were almost sacrilege to invade their thoughts. The old question of the carven Sphinx sat on each bronze face. The far cry of the hills and plains—the memories of other days—forged new lines until the brow of each solemn warrior seemed like a page in the book of fate. They saw again the slowly rising smoke column, as in the sunrise and from the far off hilltop it lifted its call for the chiefs to assemble. The memory of the old days stirred their hearts. Again they saw the flaming council fires, and heard once more the burning speech of their brothers as they counselled for war or the welfare of the tribe. The blood of youth again chased in their veins as they felt once more that they might sit in council as in the old time and then die in peace. The old war-bonnets and war-shirts were brought out; the coup stick with its trembling eagle feathers, the ancient bows and arrows. The favourite horse was blanketed, and the journey begun. Old scenes and landmarks were made new. Here they crossed a river through whose rushing waters they had, in other days, pursued a foe. Over there was a coulee where in exciting patience they had sought to ambush the enemy. Yonder was a plain that had been a battlefield. Winding over the pine-girt hilltop they traced an old buffalo trail. And now they had reached the council lodge. They had partaken of the bread and meat. They had exchanged greetings, and pledged themselves to brotherhood and peace. How familiar it all seemed! For one splendid moment they were once again really Indians. The same historic river wound its way among the purple hills and through the lacework of alder and aspen trees that like a green ribbon festooned the valley. How peaceful seemed even this place—once also a place of battle. And now the far stretch of the years loomed up: boys again, trapping foxes, learning to shoot the arrow which finally found its mark in the buffalo calf; capturing and taming the wild horse; the first war party; the first scalp, and its consequent honour among the tribe; the first coup counted; the eagle that was shot to get the coveted feather that to all men should be a pledge of victory; then the love for an Indian maiden, the ponies and furs and beadwork willingly given in exchange for this new love; the making of a new home. Thoughts of war parties, and war's bitter struggles; other coups counted, other scalps taken, were thoughts that lighted new altar fires. In imagination vast herds of ponderous buffalo once again thundered across the plains, and the exhilaration of the chase quickened the pulse beat, only to give place to the tireless lament that the buffalo were all gone. Memories of tribal tragedies, of old camping places, of the coming of the white man, of broken treaties, of the advent of the soldiers—all thronged for recognition; the wigwam around which happy children and the merry round of life sped on, the old men, their counsellors and friends, who had gone into the spirit land, and now this was to be the last, the very last council. The heart grows tense with emotion as they break the silence, and in Indian fashion chief looks into the face of chief, and, without an uttered word, they pass one by one through the doorway that leads to a land without a horizon.

The Fading Sunset

The prairie grass turned to brown, the trees on the banks of the nearby river turning to crimson and orange, the Syrian blue of the skies, holding here and there a mountainous cloud, the brilliant sunshine of the early autumn day, all served to emphasize and revivify the splendid mosaic of colouring worn by the chieftains, as, without the mockery of speech, they mounted their horses, and faced their final destiny.

The Indian is a superb horseman. Both horse and rider seem to have grown together. It is poetry in motion. The brilliant cavalcade are fast leaving the old council lodge in the distance. The word farewell was baptized with the spirit of peace, and now as they ride forth the banner of peace floats over them. Peace is in the air. Not far hence there is a river to cross, whose waters were born amid the snows of the distant mountains, and the river bathed in sunlight utters its jubilations of peace. Like "an army with banners" they enter the shaded defile of the valley—cross the swiftly flowing stream, and pass out upon the plain. Weird and picturesque is the procession as the long line of horsemen face the loneliness of the far-flung line of desert waste— the flat and sombre serenity of sand and sage and cactus. Clouds of dust are lifted from the immensity of the arid stretches, like smoke signals to the matchless immensity of the sky. The burning haze, the molten heavens, the weird and spearlike cactus, the valiant horsemen, hold the eye. We follow their trail until they are almost lost to view in the drapery that enshrouds sand and sage and riders. There seems now to be a tragic soul roaming these infinite wilds, restless and burning with passion, the companion of storms and the herald of violent deeds.

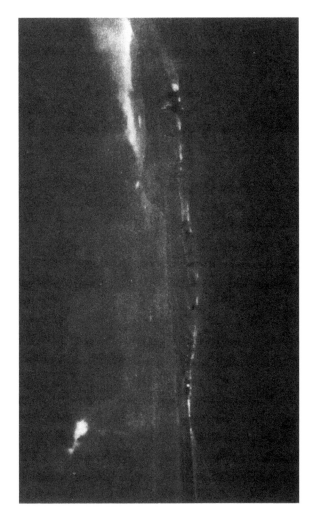

Vanishing into the Mists

The chiefs bravely emerge from these echoless silences, dust-covered but intrepid. They must now make the ascent of abrupt and massive bluffs. The summit attained, they pause for rest and retrospect. The trail has been obliterated. Every hoof-print in the sands has been erased. The trackless, yellow expanse now assumes alluring miles of colour; the royal purple of the shadows seems like tinted bands binding all the intervale back yonder to the far distant council lodge. They are familiar with the speech of the granite hills, from whose heights they now view the prospect. In these rocks, so red that it would seem as though the molten fires had not yet cooled, the Indian listens to the tongues of ten million years. Earth's heart fires had here and over there split the land and left jagged monuments of stone and red ash bearing still the tint of flame which had been cooled by the breath of countless winters. Still subject to the inner and absorbing passion of his life, the Indian made an altar in this weird sanctuary, and waited to worship.

But for the Indian the path is forever down—down into the shadowed vale, down into the abysmal canon, balustraded with sombre, cold gray rocks holding in the far recesses secret streams that make their way beneath the mountain to the cloven rock on the sunlit slope. Thither then they rode, solemn but steadfast. Once and again they turned upon their tired steeds to look back upon the far-reaching line of cliffs which to them seemed to float in the rising tide of a crimson sea. Forward and ever on until they had reached the hush of the spacious prairies, rolling like the billows of the ocean. Melancholy broods in the mind when these limitless and unexplored stretches sweep before the eye bounded only by the horizon. The spirit of a great awe stilled the souls of these men, every one, because added to the monotone of the landscape they must heed the demands for endurance, for it was again "a land where no water is." Memory is at times the birth-hour of prophecy, but here memory clothes the present with pain and loss, and for them prophecy died yesterday and the despair of a to-morrow writes its gloomy headlines upon every advance step of their journey. But the Indian will face it. He always faces death as though it were a plaything of the hour. The winds on these prairies always travel on swift wing—they are never still—they are full of spectral voices. The chiefs have left the council lodge, they have said farewell, their days of triumph are behind them. Thoughts that burn the brain held the weary pilgrims.

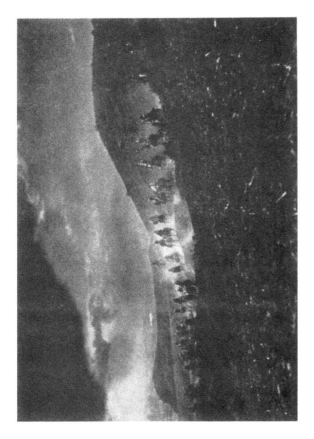

Facing the Sunset

One refreshing thought is now flung at them: their days of journeying have brought them within sight of water—water without which there is no life. That long green fringe winding under the brow of the distant hills means tree growth. The Indian loves the brotherhood of trees. Trees grow in that desolate landscape only on the borders of streams. Toward the water and welcome shade they hasten. Tired beast and tired man lave in the lifegiving flood. The horses wade in it as though the snows had melted and run thither to caress and refresh them. Oh, the exhilaration of water! On the margin of the far banks the camp is made for the night. There is witchery in a Western night. Myriads upon myriads of low-hung stars, brilliant, large and lustrous, bend to warm the soul and light the trail. Under these night lamps, amid the speech of leaves and the rush of the river, they bivouac for their last night, bending under the weight of thoughts too deep for tears. In the haze of a broken sleep they wrought out again the sorrows of their troubled record. When the morning broke through the dull gray of the eastern sky rim, he would be a heartless surgeon of emotions who attempted to probe the pathos of their thoughts, and a dull and vulgar rhetorician who should attempt to parse the fathomless sorrow of their speech.

In the hush of the new morning they mounted, and set forth upon their journey over the Great Divide. All Nature seemed conscious of the burden weighing to the earth every Indian thought, and trailing in the dust every hope of the race. The birds remembered not to sing—the prairie dogs ceased their almost continual and rasping chatter. The very horses seemed to loiter and fear the weary miles of their final day of travel. The hills, the sky, the very light of the noonday sun gathered to themselves a new atmosphere and spread it like a mantle over this travelling host. Tired feet now press the highest dome of the hills. It had been a westward climb. Full in their faces, as though to canonize the moment, the god of day had wrought cloud and sky into a miracle of sunset, transmuting by living fire the brown grasses into burnished gold—the fading sage into a silver glow, and the gleam of the distant river into the red of wine. The scene transfixed them. Gladiators of other days became helpless children. During the solemn suspense of this tragic moment, waiting in confused and wondering silence, their faces lighted with the ominous sunset sheen, one great chief uttered speech for all: "Brothers, the West, the West! We alone have the key to the West, and we must bravely unlock the portals; we can buy no lamp that will banish the night. We have always kept our time by the sun. When we pass through the gates of this dying day, we shall pass into a sunless land, and for us there shall be no more time, a forever-land of annihilating darkness."

For one wistful moment they looked and waited, then the hill upbore them no longer. They filed down the narrow, barren ridge, lined on either hand by sullen and impassable gulfs. Their eagle feathers fluttered from war-bonnet and coup stick, encarnadined by the sun's red rays. Steeper and more rugged became the path until they were confronted by the sharp edge of the bluff. There was danger in the untrodden descent. It was a pathway of struggle.

Once in the valley

>They said farewell forever.

>Thus departed the Great Chieftains,

>In the purple mists of evening.

The Sunset of a Dying Race

The Indian composes music for every emotion of his soul. He has a song for the Great Mystery; for the animals of the chase; for the maiden he woos; for the rippling river. His prayers are breathed in song. His whole life is an expression in music. These songs are treasured down through the ages, and old age teaches youth the import of the melody so that nothing is lost, nothing forgotten. Haydn wrote his "Creation," Beethoven his "Symphonies," Mendelssohn his "Songs Without Words," Handel gave the world his "Dead March in Saul," Mozart was commissioned by Count Walsegg to pour his great soul into a requiem; during its composition he felt that he was writing the dead march of his soul. For generations it has been sung in the little church at St. Mark's, where the great composer lies in an unknown grave. Had the Indian the combined soul of these masters in music, could he cull from symphony and oratorio and requiem and dirge the master notes that have thrilled and inspired the ages, he then would falter at the edge of his task in an attempt to register the burden of his lament, and utter for the generations of men the requiem wrought out during these moments of passion—a passion of sorrow so sad that the voice of it must ride through the width of the sky, and conquer the thunder of the fiercest tempest. The orchestral grandeur of the world's great composers is the child of genius. They reached the far heights of inspiration in a few isolated instances and for the delight of men. The Indian composing his own requiem must encompass the eternal pathos of a whole race of mankind riding forth beyond the challenge of death. It is well that the Indian does not compose this death march, for the sorrow of it would hush all lullabies, and banish the laughter of children.

Napoleon said to his soldiers, drawn up in battle line on the plains of Egypt, in sight of the solemn Sphinx and the eternal pyramids: "Forty centuries look down upon your actions to-day!" Four hundred and a score years ago Columbus looked first upon the red man. These solemn centuries look down upon this day; look down upon the sheathed sword, the broken coup stick, the shattered battle-axe, the deserted wigwams, the last red men mobilized on the plains of death. Ninety millions, with suffused eyes, watch this vanishing remnant of a race, whose regnant majesty inspires at the very moment it succumbs to the iconoclasm of civilization. It is the imposing triumph of solitary grandeur sweeping beyond the reach of militant crimes, their muffled footfalls reaching beyond the margin of an echo.

The Empty Saddle

Milton Keynes UK
Ingram Content Group UK Ltd.
UKHW030837021124
450589UK00006B/708